Banners for Worship

Carol Jean Harms

CONCORDIA PUBLISHING HOUSE · SAINT LOUIS

To my husband, Dr. Leonard Harms; to my mother and father, Emma and George Polack; to my children, Joel, Joy, Kenneth, Kendra, and Kelly; and to my sister, Billie Lou Kober. God bless them all.

Library of Congress Cataloging-in-Publication Data
Harms, Carol Jean, 1940-
    Banners for worship.
    1. Church pennants. I. Title.
BV168.F5H37 1988   264'.0028   88-1033
ISBN 0-570-04492-8

    14 15 16 17 18 19 20   11 10 09 08 07 06

Contents

Introduction

Both the novice and experienced banner maker will benefit from the basic guidelines and clever techniques developed by author Carol Jean Harms and her mother Emma Polack. It was she who perfected a unique way of using a cutting board, pins, and yardsticks to position design pieces and letters easily and accurately on background fabric. Both women have experimented with newer items on the market that take some of the struggle out of assembling banners, specifically, paper backed fusing web and freezer wrap paper for convenience in tracing and handling design pieces, and a walking foot attachment used for topstitching or quilting. The author introduces the novel method of using double stick tape to combine the backgrounds, emblems, and words so that the banners become more versatile.

The widely varied designs include something for banner makers of all tastes and experience. The clearly drawn illustrations make it easy for the beginner to select and follow a suitable pattern. Guidelines for arranging the composition enable those with more expertise to tailor a banner to fit a particular purpose. And the additional information section invites anyone to create new banners using ideas of their own.

The banner designs are adaptable to other purposes as well. A combination of fabrics and paper, for instance, would make an exciting visual aid hanging in a classroom or hallway. An overhead projector can enlarge the emblems, designs, and letter patterns to fit any size space.

Banners for Worship is divided into several major sections—

GENERAL INSTRUCTIONS: introduces all the basic materials and methods necessary for preparing a banner. **Read this section before starting a banner.** Note those techniques or rules that apply especially to the making of a particular design.

DESIGN PATTERNS: Includes 105 color-coded banner designs with variations, and 6 complete, interchangeable alphabet patterns.

DESIGN INFORMATION: provides specific production techniques, explains the content, and suggests alternate uses for each banner design.
For easy use, the book offers additional special features—

BANNER INDEX: groups the banner designs according to major liturgical themes.

COLOR KEY: shows the color of the numbered areas of the graphed designs. This back-of-the-book chart is intended to be a convenient reference for use when purchasing materials.

General Instructions

PREPARATIONS

Assembling Equipment

☐ BANNER SUPPLY BOX

Obtain a large cardboard box (with an optional lid) that will hold most of the banner equipment. This banner supply box is easy to store until the next banner is made. Assemble the smaller, easy-to-lose items in ziplock bags and clear plastic containers with lids. Label any containers which are not transparent.

If space is available in the work area it is a convenience to have a movable kitchen serving cart to hold the banner supply box and any other items needed for making the banners.

This book offers a variety of techniques for preparing a banner. Therefore select (✔) those items from each category below that will be utilized for the method chosen.

☐ CUTTING UTENSILS

SCISSORS: a pair for cutting large pieces of fabric; a pair for cutting paper; a small pair for cutting out letters or difficult corners (usually kept in the letter box).

ROTARY CUTTER WITH PLASTIC MAT

X-ACTO KNIFE

☐ MARKING UTENSILS

CHALK PENCILS: both blue and white.

PENCIL

SLIVERS OF SOAP

TRACING WHEEL and **TRACING PAPER**

FELT-TIP MARKERS: any dark colors.

PERMANENT BLACK FELT-TIP MARKER

HI-LITER MARKERS or **OIL CRAYONS**

RULERS: 6″; 12″; any size clear plastic ruler preferably with grid markings; L-shaped.

YARDSTICKS: one with a hole in one end; one of metal; one longer than 36″ (or a lattice stick).

LARGE, WOODEN COMPASS

GRAPHED ACETATE SHEET: marked with ¼″ grid lines.

(The 8½″ by 11″ clear plastic sheet can be laid over any design that is to be enlarged. Lam-I-Graphs can be purchased wherever quilting and needlepoint supplies are sold. Or, write to Extra Special Products, Box 777, Greenville, OH 45331.)

☐ PAPER

FREEZER WRAP: 18″ wide roll.

MYLAR: gold and silver mirrored plastic film sold by the yard at art, retail display, or florist shops.

COLORED FOIL: as called for, from the florist.

TRACING PAPERS: gift wrap tissue paper, wax paper (requires crayons or grease pencil for marking), tissue from old dress patterns, newsprint (from a moving company), paper with 1″ markings (found at some fabric stores), or Pellon.

☐ FABRICS/TRIMS

BLACK RUG YARN

BLACK FELT: one to three yards of soft, black felt.

TRIM BOX: scraps of trim, ribbon, fringe, foil, and mylar of varying length, width, and color for experimenting with the composition.

ZIPLOCK BAG WITH YARN AND FELT LETTER SAMPLES: containing several 2' lengths of black rug yarn and the letters S, A, T, and O cut from felt scraps in black, white, red, or any other colors that might be used on a banner; to take to the store when shopping for fabrics.

☐ BONDING MATERIALS

CLOTH TAPE: different widths for different needs.

SCOTCH DOUBLE STICK CELLOPHANE TAPE

SCOTCH DOUBLE STICK CARPET TAPE: found wherever carpet supplies are sold.

Q-TIPS

CRAFT GLUES: (suitable for fabric) thin, clear drying such as Slomons' Sobo Glue; thick, clear drying such as Aleene's All Purpose Tacky Glue.

ALEENE'S FINE LINE SYRINGE AND GLUE APPLICATOR: applies thick glue in a very fine line.

GLUE GUN

RUBBER CEMENT

FUSIBLE INTERFACING

PELLON WONDER-UNDER: paper-backed fusing web.

STITCH WITCHERY: fusible web.

KITCHEN PARCHMENT PAPER: 18" wide roll.

EASY WAY APPLIQUE PRESSING SHEET: a teflon sheet for applying fusible web to the back of fabric.

(If this product cannot be found at a fabric store then write to Solar-Kist Corporation, Crafts Division, PO Box 273, LaGrange, IL 60525.)

☐ PRODUCTION ITEMS

CUTTING BOARD: cardboard, folding with a grid of printed lines 1" apart (the kind used for cutting out fabric).

BALL HEAD PINS

MAGNETIC PIN HOLDER

SUPPLIES FOR HANGING THE BANNER: cords, chains, tacks, decorative nails, etc.

LARGE PAPER BAG

ZIPLOCK BAGS: heavy-duty, freezerweight.

PRESSING CLOTH

STEAM IRON and **IRONING BOARD**

LATTICE STICKS or **DOWELS:** various sizes according to need.

MASTER GRID: a large, homemade graph sheet for enlarging patterns.

(Cut a piece of paper 34" x 60". Line up the edges with the vertical and horizontal lines on the cutting board. Push a ball head pin into each corner of the paper to keep it from slipping. Place the yardstick on the lines of the cutting board and with a black marker draw a line every 2" until the enlarged graph is complete.)

☐ LETTER BOX

A small cardboard box or plastic tub is used for all the supplies needed for making letters: a small pair of scissors with sharp pointed tips; pencil; chalk pencil; soap sliver; 6″ ruler; rubber cement; file folders; ziplock bags; paper bag; and sheets of freezer paper.

Along with the letter box carry a **lap board** (perhaps an old cookie sheet with edges) that has a smooth, hard surface for tracing and corduroy at one end to keep the letters from slipping. This equipment may be conveniently used whenever there is time to sit and cut, such as while watching television or attending a meeting.

Most of the supplies needed may be found wherever sewing, craft, art, or school supplies are sold. Check the florist for ribbon, metallic paper, or foil. Look in the advertisements of craft and sewing magazines for catalogs that sell trim in bulk quantities at lower prices. For a free catalog which offers a limited variety of inexpensive trim, ribbon, and tracing paper, write to Newark Dressmaker Supply, 6473 Ruch Road, P.O. Box 2448 Dept. D4, Lehigh Valley, PA 18001.

Enlarging the Design

First divide the design to be enlarged into ¼″ squares either by taping a graphed acetate sheet over it or by drawing lines directly on the page with pencil and ruler.

Check to see if the church or local school has an opaque or overhead projector and thermofax machine available. If so, cut paper to the finished banner size and attach it to a smooth wall surface. With an opaque projector the image is cast directly from the book's pattern onto the wall. If using an overhead projector the design's pattern must first be traced onto an acetate sheet with a special pen such as Sanford's Vis à Vis pen. Use a thermofax machine if possible. It will make a direct copy of the book's banner design onto an acetate sheet. To save on expenses place as many designs as possible onto one sheet for copying by the thermofax.

When projecting the image onto the wall adjust the machine so the image fits the paper exactly and then trace. Make a second tracing of those sections of the pattern which will be pinned to the fabric and cut. To save time trace several banner patterns in one session. **Do not use a felt-tip marker on paper unless there is a protective backing to keep the ink from bleeding through to the surface below.**

If no projector is available then use the master grid to make a full-size pattern. Place the paper (cut to the exact dimensions as indicated on the design) on top of the master grid. Sketch the enlarged design with the scale of one (¼″) square on the book's design equal to the 2″ square on the master grid. If the paper is not transparent enough to see the grid lines while working on a table then tape the master grid and paper to a window and enlarge the design that way.

A master grid may be marked directly onto a cutting board using a yardstick and a permanent black felt-tip marker. Retrace only those lines which are 2″ apart, i.e., 2″, 4″, 6″, 8″, etc. Use freezer or other nonopaque paper for enlarging the designs.

Use a large, wooden compass to enlarge a circle when using the master grid. If a large compass is not available then make one as illustrated below.

Place the eraser end of a pencil in the hole at one end of a yardstick which then becomes the pivot point for the circle. Measure the circle's radius from the hole to the edge of the yardstick where the other pencil will mark the line. Hold the eraser in place at the pivot point and rotate the outer pencil to mark the circle on the paper pattern.

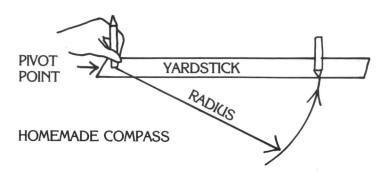

Selecting Background Fabrics

Choose fabrics for the background that are heavy enough to provide adequate body for hanging without buckling or curling. The best materials for this would be upholstery velvets, heavy or firm drapery material, corduroy (ribbed, or uncut which looks like velvet), woven-backed velveteen, linen, Monks cloth, heavy cotton, felt, and 100% polyester craft felt (which has a hard, smooth finish). White, satin-finish drapery material with rubberized backing is an excellent choice because no hem or lining is required.

Avoid knits, stretchy fabrics, gabardine weaves, and inexpensive burlap. Glue and double stick tape do not adhere to polyester felt and fabrics. Only fusible web, fusible interfacing, and rubber cement will bond to polyester.

Fusible interfacing (medium or heavyweight) will provide extra body for thin, woven fabrics and keep softer rayon and wool felt from stretching out of shape. Satin and similar fabrics can be used if treated with special care. For fabrics that react adversely to moisture use Wonder-Under.

Estimating Size and Yardage

Use the following formula for estimating the banner's **Length Allowance:**

1. Finished length of banner

plus

2. Top hem allowance
   a) Allow twice the width of the lattice stick or three times the dowel's diameter.
   b) If uncertain of the size rod being used, allow 3″ extra.
   c) If using cut loops, allow for the extra inches.

plus

3. Bottom hem allowance
   a) Allow extra material for adding a hem (½" to 1"), a fringe, a rod, or cut loops.
   b) No allowance is needed if the bottom is left as a cut edge.
   c) Allow 3" if uncertain of how to finish the bottom.

Use the following formula for estimating the **Width Allowance:**

1. Finished width of banner

plus

2. Side hem allowance
   a) Allow ½" to 1" on each side.
   b) No allowance is needed if the sides are left as cut edges.

If the fabric is wide enough for the banner's length then purchase the piece according to the banner's width. Also consider the following factors when estimating yardage:

1. Add 2" or more to compensate for cutting error.

2. Allow enough fabric to have scrap pieces for testing shrinking, gluing, and fusing.

3. If the banner is to be washable, allow for preshrinking loss.

4. Allow 2" or 3" extra per side of banner if it is to be quilted.

5. When lining with self-fabric, purchase twice the length of the banner plus 8".

Take this book along to the fabric store. The designs will be of help in estimating the exact amount of material needed for each color and for the words. The **yardage chart,** and the **color key,** are handy to have along when purchasing fabrics.

Selecting the Colors

□ AT THE STORE

The designs in this book are color keyed by number to the chart located on the back cover. Color substitution may be necessary if the colors cannot be matched exactly. For example, blues 21, 24, and 25 in the color key, called for in a given banner, may not be available. Then select another suitable combination of three blues that harmonizes with the remaining colors in the banner.

Find a place in the store where several bolts of fabric can be laid next to each other. Include any swatches brought from home for matching. Arrange the colors the same way they will appear in the design. Lay the 2' strands of black rug yarn (stored in the ziplock bag) along the edges between adjoining colors. Then lay the sample felt letters (also stored in the ziplock bag) on the colors that will be the background for the words. Stand back as far as possible from the arrangement to evaluate its total effect. Keep adjusting the materials until the best possible appearance is achieved.

Check to see whether the letters lose legibility when viewed from a distance. For example, the recommended black letters which do not offer enough contrast to be easily read on the selected violet background may be replaced with letters of white or one of the other colors from the banner. Or, a recommended yellow that disappears on a white background may be replaced with a deeper yellow that offers a greater contrast and still goes with the rest of the banner.

Plan ahead and purchase seasonal colors when they are available. It is difficult to find bright yellows in the autumn and dark violets in the spring.

☐ COLOR THEORY

The following basic facts about the properties of color are valuable for the banner maker to remember when selecting an alternate color combination for the given banners or when creating an altogether new design.

Color has value, intensity, and temperature (warm or cool). Generally the colors which are high in value and intensity and are warm attract the eye first and will be the center of interest in a design. **Warm colors** come forward, making objects look larger and closer. Yellow, yellow-orange, and red are warm. **Cool colors** recede in the design, making objects look smaller and farther away. Blue, blue-green, green, violet, and blue-violet are cool in appearance. For example, in choosing a red to be used for the focal point, an orange-red will be warmer and attract attention more than the cooler violet-red.

Value is the degree of lightness and darkness in a color. The following chart illustrates the relative value of colors:

COLOR	VALUE
YELLOW	LIGHT
YELLOW-ORANGE, YELLOW-GREEN	
ORANGE, GREEN	
RED-ORANGE, BLUE-GREEN	MIDDLE
RED, BLUE	
RED-VIOLET, BLUE-VIOLET	
VIOLET	DARK

For example, a bright yellow will always look light. Even the brightest violet will be dark. An ochre (darkened yellow) does not show well on blue. There is not enough contrast in values. Yellow-green and ochre felt letters will not show up against some low value backgrounds.

A **tint** (a higher value version of a color), commonly known as a pastel, is made by adding white dye to the original color. The more white added the cooler the color becomes. A **shade** (a lower value version of a color) is made by adding black dye to the original color. This also makes a color cooler.

Intensity is the degree of brightness or dullness. Rainbow colors are the brightest and highest in intensity. When white, black, or grey dyes are added to the rainbow colors their intensity is lowered or dulled. Thus tints and shades have lower intensities. A color is also dulled or greyed when its complimentary color (the color opposite it on the color wheel) is added.

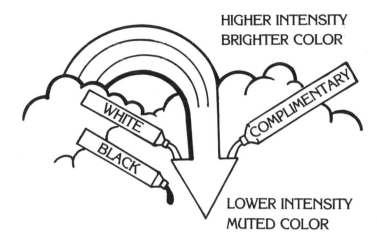

HIGHER INTENSITY
BRIGHTER COLOR

LOWER INTENSITY
MUTED COLOR

Banners with brilliant colors of nearly equal intensity look terrific. Do not mix dull, faded, or pastel colors with bright ones. Pastel colors are appropriate on chocolate brown or dark, dense blue or green. Black and white are neutral and go with all colors.

Rule of Thumb: Use no more than three colors (including their tints, shades, and related colors) **plus black and white.** Related colors are those adjacent to a color on the color wheel, e.g., yellow-orange and yellow-green are related to yellow. Thus a banner may have a color combination of blues, violets, and yellows (including possibly ochre, yellow-orange, and yellow-green) plus black and white. Do not add the fourth color of red(s).

☐ COLOR WHEEL

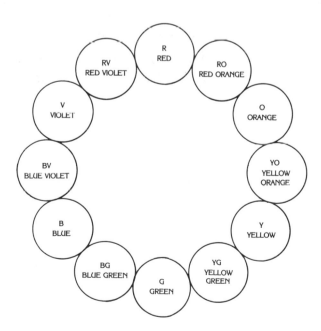

If there is a need for using alternate colors on a banner, then make several tracings of the design and color with markers or crayons until the desired effect is achieved. Following is a list of color combinations that are attractive on banners:

Monochromatic colors are different shades of one color. A banner composed of light blue, medium blue, and dark blue, for instance, would have a quiet appearance.

Complimentary colors are the colors opposite each other on the color wheel (R—G B—O V—Y BV—YO RO—BG RV—YG). Following are examples of complimentary colors used successfully:

1. A splash of green intensifies a large red area (Banner 20).

2. Equal areas of juxtaposed complimentary colors such as blue and orange vibrate (Banner 28).

3. Brilliant compliments such as violet and yellow combined with black and white make a striking combination (Banner 29).

Analogous colors are families of colors related to each other by being mixed with a common color.

The following are examples:

Yellow Family: Y YO YG O G

Green Family: G YG BG

Violet Family: V RV BV

Orange Family: O RO YO

Blue Family: B BV BG V G

Red Family: R RV RO V O

Split-complimentary colors consist of a color plus the colors adjacent to its compliment on the color wheel. The following are examples:

Y—RV—BV V—YG—YO

B—YO—RO G—RV—RO

R—YG—BG O—BG—BV

Triad colors are any three colors equidistant from each other on the color wheel (for instance, Y—B—R V—G—O YG—BV—RO). The effect is brilliant and eye-catching when combined with black or white.

☐ ASSOCIATIONS WITH COLOR

Throughout the Christian Church's history certain colors have become associated with the major and minor festivals, special occasions, and seasons of the church year as indicated below.

Advent—violet or blue

New Year's Eve/Day—white

Epiphany—white (second through eighth Sundays—green)

Transfiguration of Our Lord—white

Ash Wednesday—violet or black

Lent—violet

Palm Sunday—scarlet or violet

Maundy Thursday—scarlet or white

Good Friday—black

Easter—white (Easter Day—white or gold)

Pentecost—red

Trinity Sunday—white

season after Pentecost—green

Reformation Day—red

All Saints' Day—white

Thanksgiving Day—white

Check with the minister for a calendar that designates the color for each Sunday.

In the western world colors also have had traditional associations with the following themes:

blue—hope, love, truth, faithfulness, heaven

white—purity, holiness, innocence, faith, light

violet—royalty, repentance, remorse

black—sin, death, evil

scarlet—royalty, loyalty

red—fire, love

green—growth, victory, hope

gold—God's abundance, marriage

CONSTRUCTION TECHNIQUES

Preparing the Background

Make sure the fabric hangs and is cut on the straight of the grain. Use the lines of the cutting board and yardsticks to measure the border accurately. Double check the direction of napped materials before cutting. Allow extra fabric for the top rod and any hems or tabs used.

If possible shrink the background fabric before the material is cut, or else the moisture from the glue and the steam iron (especially when applying fusible web or interfacing) may cause puckering. Felt, rubber backed fabrics, and upholstery materials do not need to be preshrunk. Shrink fabrics by machine washing and drying or by pressing with a wet cloth. Steam ironing will not completely shrink the fabric.

Dip fusible interfacing and delicate fabrics into warm water being careful not to create wrinkles. Lay the fabric flat between towels and pat gently to absorb the excess moisture. Hang to air dry. **If in doubt, do a test piece first.**

Lining the Background Piece

If a fabric for the background is too lightweight to hang properly then line it using one of the following methods:

1. Apply **fusible interfacing** (preshrink) to the back. No hems are needed on the bottom and sides.

2. Cut a lining of **heavy fabric** the same size as the background. Allow for a top hem to accomodate a rod. The edges are glued or fused with ¾" strips of Stitch Witchery.

3. Follow method 2 only press the hem and secure with a few dots of glue first. Cut a **lining slightly smaller** and attach it to the banner.

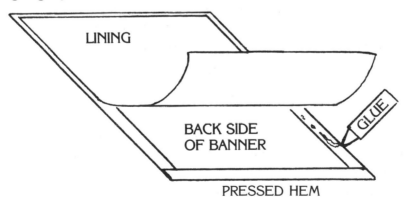

LINING

BACK SIDE OF BANNER

PRESSED HEM

4. Use Pellon Wonder-Under to bond a lining to the banner. The banner and its lining are made from **one piece.** This is the best way to line satin and similar fabrics because steam is not used. Purchase twice the length of the banner plus 8". Cut off a 6" strip from one end. Fold the rest of the fabric (wrong sides together) in half so the selvages match. Press the center fold line which becomes the top of the banner. Use the cutting board and yardsticks to measure and mark the width of the banner plus 1". From the center fold, measure and mark the banner's length plus ½". Pin the

edges together to keep the fabric pieces from sliding while trimming away
the excess fabric. Remove the pins. Unfold the fabric so the wrong side is
up. Cut Wonder-Under to fit the exact width and add 3″ to the length. The
3″ extends beyond the center line. Fuse the paper-backed web and peel off
the paper. Center the 6″ strip over the fold line so 3″ is on each side of it.
Fuse the strip. Fold the fabric (wrong sides together), align the edges,
carefully smooth out any ripples, and fuse. Trim away the excess fabric on
the sides and bottom. The fused edge of the banner will not ravel with
careful handling. A rod can be slipped through the 3″ opening on the fold
line.

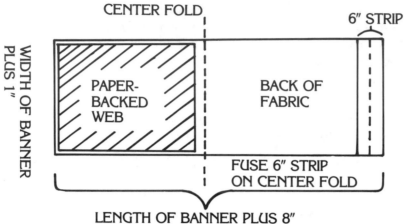

5. When using method 4 to fuse a **separate piece** of fabric as a lining, purchase the length of the banner plus 4″. Fuse the two materials together.
Trim away excess fabric on the sides and bottom of the banner. Fold the
top 3″ to form a hem on the back to accomodate a rod. Glue the hem in
place.

Finishing the Sides and Gluing
Raw Edges

Finish the sides of the banner first unless special attention is required for
doing tabs. If the fabric has a nonfraying edge leave the cut edge as the
border. Three ways to stabilize a raveling edge with glue follow:

1. Apply a thin line of glue with a toothpick or a Q-tip.

2. Dab some glue onto a fingertip and pull it along the back edge of the
fabric.

3. Mark the border for the sides and bottom on the back of the banner.
Spread rubber cement (using the jar's applicator) directly over the marked
border. When the cement dries cut along the line. Do a sample first.

Some fabrics will look neater if hemmed. Press under ½″ to 1″ for a hem.
Secure with glue or fuse with ½″ strips of Stitch Witchery. If using an applied border on the sides, determine if it might be better to glue the trimming material on before finishing the top and bottom of the banner.

Applied Borders

Generally the width of applied borders will vary from ⅜″ to ⅞″. The recommended width and color for a banner's borders are flexible (considering,

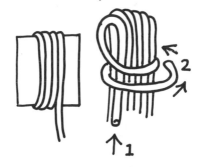

for instance, that there might be a terrific buy on ⅝″ velvet ribbon). If the walls are very dark then black may not be the best color for a border. Substitute white or a dominant color in the design or a color complimentary to the main color used. If a white background does not show well against a white or light colored wall then add a border of black rug yarn or ⅜″ (or any suitable width) black ribbon or felt strips to help the banner stand out from its surroundings. Experiment with different colored ribbons from the sample box if substitution is necessary.

A ribbon attached with double stick tape may be changed as suggested for Banner 66. The ribbon can then easily be pulled off and replaced with a different colored one as needed.

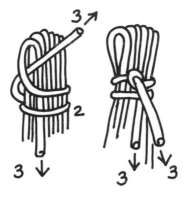

Finishing the Bottom

There is no need for a dowel at the bottom of a banner when using fabrics that have adequate body or a lining. If the banner does not hang well after it is completed add a stick to the back at the bottom with cloth tape.

Adding Fringe

Finish the bottom edge in the same manner as the sides. Four methods for applying fringe follow:

1. Buy fringe at the store and glue or sew it in place.

2. Make loop fringe from yarn.

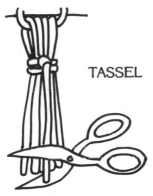

TASSEL

3. Make a yarn or ⅛″ ribbon fringe which is stitched to the bottom of the banner with a yarn needle. No hem is necessary. Use a thin line of glue on the raw edge to retard any raveling. Experiment first to determine the length of the loops (which are cut in half and pulled into knotted strands) and the distance between the finished strands. Measure and mark the distance between each knot. Stitch continuous loops of yarn or ribbon across the bottom edge. Cut the loops in half as illustrated. Use a crochet hook to pull the center loop down from the back. Then hook and pull through the two front strands, gently tightening the knot. Trim the fringe's edge to a uniform length.

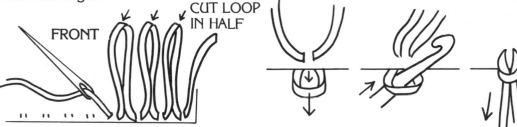

FRONT   CUT LOOP IN HALF

4. Unravel the horizontal threads from the bottom of the banner leaving the vertical threads to create a fringe of at least 3″ (A). Allow for extra fabric. Run a thin line of glue along the back to hold the bottom horizontal threads in place. It is possible to create one or more narrow bands of pulled threads near the bottom fringe (B). If making very long fringe the threads may be evenly divided and tied together (C).

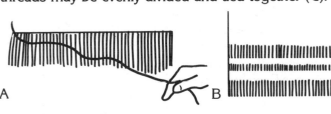

A   B   C

5. On a separate piece of fabric pull threads to the desired length leaving a 2″ woven band at the top. Pin the band into position on the back of the banner, check that the band is not visible from the front, and adjust for evenness and length. The fringe may be just as long as the banner or hang several inches below it. Glue or fuse the band in place. If the fringe is to be removable then attach with cloth tape or double stick carpet tape. The fringe can enhance any shape banner base.

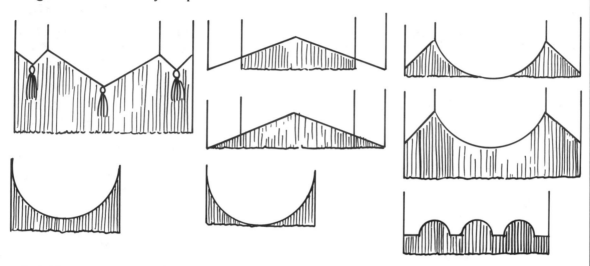

Adding a New Shape to the Banner's Base

Illustrated below are various alternate shapes for the bottom of a banner. Be sure the shape chosen harmonizes with the lines of the banner's design. Allow extra fabric for any changes made. Banner bases using separate side bans of contrasting or harmonizing colors are shown on Banner A3.

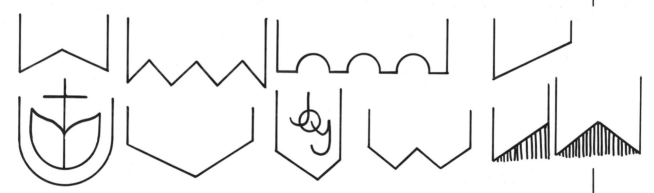

Finishing the Top Edge

The top edge of the banner is finished last. Measure and fold the top hem allowing enough room for a lattice stick or rod to slide through easily. If in doubt as to the size and kind of rod to be used allow 3″ for the top hem. To prevent the fabric from raveling, pink the edge, or run a line of glue along the raw edge, or, if sewing, turn the top edge down ¼″ before finishing the hem. No hem is required for the top edge when the banner is tacked onto a lattice stick and hung with nails as shown on Banner A3.

Making Tabs (Loops)

The tab (cut loop) is a popular treatment for the top and/or bottom of banners. The designs in this book do not necessarily need additional treatment such as tabs or fringe. Be careful that such embellishments will enhance the banner's design rather than detract from it.

Purchase extra fabric for tabs on the top and/or bottom of the banner. The width of the banner will determine the number of loops needed to adequately support its weight and prevent sagging. Make the tabs and the spaces between them approximately the same width. If possible sew or glue the top and bottom edges the same way when using rods at both ends. To keep the cut edges from raveling run a thin line of glue along the raw edge, line the fabric with fusible interfacing, or line the area with self-fabric using Wonder-Under before cutting the tabs.

Following are three ways of doing **tabs using self-fabric:**

Handling loops and background fabric **as one piece**—A side hem may be unnecessary if the fabric is nonraveling. Allow approximately 7" for the top and 7" for the bottom when the tabs and background are cut as one piece.

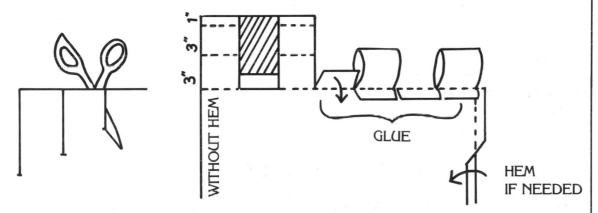

Bottom edge **without a rod**—Allow 3" or more for tabs cut into the bottom edge of the background fabric.

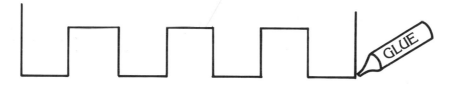

Loop pieces **separately cut** and sewn to the background—Use an extra 8" at the top and 8" at the bottom for 3" foldover tabs.

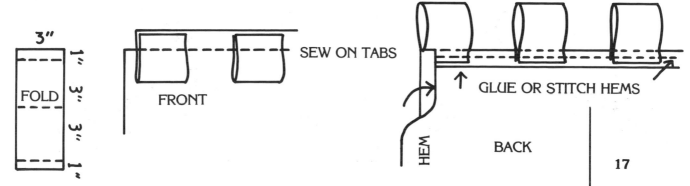

Tabs of a contrasting or harmonizing color act as a border for the top and/or bottom of a banner. The following illustrations show how these tabs may be glued to the banner.

GLUE INDIVIDUAL TABS OR A STRIP OF TABS TO THE BASE OF THE BANNER. FRONT OR BACK OF BANNER

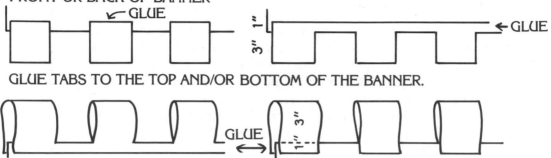

GLUE TABS TO THE TOP AND/OR BOTTOM OF THE BANNER.

Gluing and Fusing

Use the chart to determine which bonding methods work best with assorted fabrics and trim. Then experiment to find the most suitable, convenient, and/or economical method to use for a particular banner. **Always do a test piece first.**

KEY
✔: recommended for use
♥: best method for that kind of fabric or trim
A: apply sparingly to avoid puckering or bleeding
B: test for bleeding first
P: page to consult for more information

GLUING AND FUSING CHART

	SATIN AND SIMILAR FABRICS	HEAVY FABRIC, FELT	THIN FABRIC	POLYESTER FELT AND FABRIC	RIBBON	RUG YARN	LETTERS	METALLIC PAPER, FOIL, FABRIC
THIN GLUE P19		✔		WILL NOT BOND	B	✔ P23–24	✔	
THICK GLUE P19	✔ A B P19	✔	✔ A B	WILL NOT BOND	♥ B	✔ P23–24	✔	✔
SYRINGE GLUE APPLICATOR P6	✔ P19		✔	WILL NOT BOND	✔	✔	✔	
RUBBER CEMENT		✔	B	✔ B P22	✔ B		✔ P25	✔ P19, 21
FUSIBLE WEB	✔ P20	✔	✔	♥	✔		✔ P20	
FUSIBLE INTERFACING P20		TO LINE FELT	✔ FOR LINING	✔ P22			✔ FOR LINING	
GLUE GUN		✔		✔ P22			✔	
DOUBLE STICK TAPE P6				WILL NOT BOND	✔ P15		✔ P26	✔ TEST FIRST
PAPER-BACKED FUSING WEB P20	♥ P20, 13	✔	✔	♥ P22	✔		✔ P20, 32	✔ TEST FIRST

□ BONDING TECHNIQUES

GLUE: Thin glue is the easiest to use, but it will also readily form blobs. Practice drawing an even line of glue. Be aware that the higher moisture content of thin glue is more apt to cause bleeding and puckering. Thick glue is more versatile but hard to squeeze from the bottle.

Bleeding occurs when too much glue is used and it soaks through to the front surface leaving a shiny spot. To correct this problem try using thick glue applied with a fingertip or syringe glue applicator, or rubber cement.

Puckering occurs when moisture from the glue or a steam iron slightly shrinks the fabric. To remedy this problem try (a) preshrinking the fabric, (b) using rubber cement, or (c) applying thick glue sparingly with a fingertip or syringe glue applicator.

Accidental drops of glue will leave shiny spots on a banner. If the fabric will not waterspot or shrink then remove the glue immediately with a damp cloth. To avoid this problem, **cover all but the immediate area of the banner being glued.**

To reattach a loose edge spread glue on the end of a 1″ by 3″ strip cut from a cereal box. Slip the strip under the loose edge and slide it along until the area is moistened. Remove the strip and press the edge down. **Note:** A design piece that is pinned in position (but not glued yet) may be glued to the banner in this same manner.

Check the sewing notions department for new glues that would be economical and suitable for bonding fabrics. Test for bleeding, shrinking, discoloration, convenience, and bondability for specific fabrics before using.

RUBBER CEMENT: Test rubber cement on a sample of fabric.

Rubber cement does not have the moisture of glue and therefore does not cause puckering from shrinkage. It will bond **nonfabric materials.**

To reduce the usual messiness of rubber cement, have **two jars.** In the bottom of the first jar maintain a level of cement of about ½″ which will keep the applicator's stem dry. Use this bottle for doing all of the cementing. Use the second jar to refill the first jar as needed.

Check to see whether or not the cement bleeds. Let the cement thoroughly dry first (wait several minutes). If the rubber cement is too runny or bleeding occurs then set the open jar outside until enough moisture evaporates to achieve the **consistency** desired for spreading without bleeding.

If the cement is too thick and leaves unsightly blobs under the fabric, then press the straight edge of a ruler down and out towards the edge (in a scraping motion) forcing out the **excess cement.** Allow it to dry, then gently rub it from the banner.

If a drop of cement accidentally falls on the banner let the cement dry and gently rub it off with a finger. If the cement is spread on with the jar's applicator then it cannot be fully rubbed off permanently discoloring the fabric.

After a cemented design piece is laid in place it is possible to lift and reposition it. Be careful that a stain is not left on the banner in the process of shifting the piece. Puckering of fabric along the edge is easy to smooth out by pressing with the fingers.

FUSIBLE INTERFACING: Fusible interfacing (medium or heavyweight) is used to line felt, lightweight backgrounds, and white and light colored design pieces that are used on a dark background and to prevent woven fabrics from raveling.

Preshrink the interfacing (and if possible the other fabric as well) to avoid uneven shrinking problems when fusing.

FUSIBLE WEB: Though more expensive to use than glue, this material is excellent for **stabilizing fabric.**

1. **Pellon Wonder-Under**, a paper backed fusing web, makes this easy. To trace a design piece or letter mark it on the right side of the fabric, reverse the pattern and trace it on the Wonder-Under paper side, or use the fusible web/freezer wrap method described below.

Place Wonder-Under rough (web) side down on the wrong side of the fabric. Press for 3 seconds or less with an iron (dry, medium or hot setting). Continue until every inch of the web is pressed. Always lift the iron to the next position. **Never slide the iron or press too long.** For felt use lower heat and less pressing time. Do a test piece first. Let the fabric cool, cut out the design piece, gently peel off the paper, and fuse the piece of fabric to the background. (The Wonder-Under paper backing, once peeled from the fused web, can be used again with Stitch Witchery for other design pieces.) Use this method for satin banners.

To reverse the pattern, tape the banner sketch with its front to a window. Position Wonder-Under (web side down) on the back of the taped sheet and trace the lines.

2. Substitute **Stitch Witchery and kitchen parchment paper** for Wonder-Under. Sandwich Stitch Witchery between the back of the fabric and parchment paper. Continue as for method 1.

3. The **least expensive** method is also the most tedious. Trace the pattern onto the right side of the fabric. Stitch Witchery may be applied to the back by holding a steam iron ½" above the web until it barely melts into the material. **Do not overmelt.** Cut and fuse the piece to the background.

4. The last method uses a **teflon (Easy Way Applique Pressing) sheet.** Trace the pattern on the right side of the fabric. The fusible web is sandwiched between the wrong side of the fabric and the sheet. Follow the directions for Wonder-Under. This method is time-consuming if the sheet purchased is slightly larger in size than the iron.

FUSIBLE WEB/FREEZER WRAP: If using Wonder-Under or Stitch Witchery/parchment, first press on the paper-backed web (but, do not peel off the paper). Next press the freezer paper pattern onto the right side of the fabric. Cut out the piece and peel off the two papers before fusing to the background. This method may be more convenient than tracing the design piece and letters in reverse on Wonder-Under. **This procedure is recommended for satin.**

If applying Stitch Witchery with a steam iron or a teflon sheet, press the freezer wrap pattern on first. Then apply the web to the back following the directions for methods 3 and 4 above. Cut out the design piece or letter and remove the freezer paper.

Tracing and Handling
Design Pieces

The most accurate, efficient, and timesaving method for tracing pattern pieces is to use **freezer wrap.** Place the paper (coated side down) on the full-size banner pattern and trace all the pieces leaving a little space between each. Number the pattern shapes to correspond to their traced pieces. Cut apart the pattern pieces and position them on the fabric making sure that the nap is correct. Use an **iron** (dry, wool setting) to press the freezer paper to the right side of the fabric. Use lower heat and less pressing time for felt. Do a test piece first. Cut along the traced line. Do not peel away the paper until the piece is in the correct position on the banner. Handle the paper-fabric piece carefully or the paper may pop off the fabric once it cools. The paper pattern can be pressed back onto the fabric several times.

Other means for transferring patterns to fabric include (a) using a tracing wheel and tracing paper, (b) pinning the traced pattern pieces to the fabric and cutting, and (c) tracing around the already cut pattern pieces with pencil, chalk pencil, or sliver of soap.

Felt and other nonraveling fabrics are the easiest to use for design pieces. Preshrink woven fabrics using the same methods suggested for background fabrics. Several ways to avoid raveling in woven material are:

1. Handle the cut pieces as little as possible and with great care.

2. If yarn is not glued over a raw edge then run a thin line of glue with the fingertip along the back of it.

3. Back the fabric with fusible web or fusible interfacing.

4. Do not use a gabardine weave.

The background and the design pieces should be free of wrinkles before joining.

Use rubber cement to bond metallic paper or foil to tagboard (file folder weight) first and then glue the piece to the banner.

Using Satin and Similar Fabrics

For best results combine satin with Wonder-Under. Both of these materials should be rolled when purchased onto (cardboard) tubes to prevent wrinkling. Use satin for both the background and the lining, and use Wonder-Under to fuse the assorted design pieces to the background.

An unusual, one color satin banner may be made for the home based on the design of Banner 75. The finished size of the banner is approximately 22″ by 24″. Line the banner with satin using Wonder-Under. The cut edge may be covered with ribbon, lace, or trim. **Note:** Make both the background and the design pieces of the same fabric, but run the naps in opposite directions. So placed, the material will reflect the light differently creating subtle color changes as a person moves past the banner.

Applying Shade Lines

Shade lines (indicated by dotted lines on the banner pattern) have the effect of making a white background appear more radiant. These lines are drawn approximately ⅜" wide adjacent to and touching the black outline. The dots indicate where to put a long continuous line with a marker.

☐ MARKERS

The following **pens** are useful for shade lines for the colors on the color key:

(a) hot pink (12), Sanford's Major Accent;

(b) yellow (1), Sanford's Major Accent;

(c) yellow-green (8), Sanford's Major Accent-Fluorescent;

(d) light blue (21), Flair Hot Liner.

If brand name substitutions are necessary look for the wide (¼") felt-tip pens used to highlight or mark directly over words in books. Sanford, Flair, and Dennison all have these four colors available. Use any brand marker for orange (5) and violet (16). If the above colors are not available then use oil crayons instead.

When using **oil crayons** be careful not to smear the surface when coloring the felt or handling the banner. Before storing, pin a piece of tissue paper over a crayoned area to avoid having it rub off onto another banner. Oil crayons are also useful for shading or adding more color to an area, e.g., around the rays of the sun (Banner 39), along the base of a flame (Banner 16), or in the shadows of hills (Banner 19). Practice on a scrap of fabric first. If the result is unsatisfactory have someone who is more artistic do the added coloring.

Do samples first to see what looks the best.

☐ FELT

Whenever shade lines are called for on felt, use 100% polyester craft felt (such as Phun Phelt). The felt should have a hard, smooth finish for drawing lines with a marker. Rayon and wool felt are not suitable because it is difficult to draw a solid line across their loose fibers.

Glue and double stick tape will not adhere to polyester craft felt. To handle this problem:

1. Line the felt with fusible interfacing (preshrink). This method is preferred for white or light colored design pieces (e.g., the Christmas angels in Banners 19, 24) that are placed on a dark background.

2. Use fusible web, rubber cement, or a glue gun. Draw all the lines on before using the glue gun.

If using an oil crayon or nonpermanent marker for the shade lines **do all steam pressing and fusing before the lines are marked,** because the steam may cause the lines to bleed. Do not fold, roll, or wrinkle the banner when stored. Touch up ironing could be disastrous.

Assembling the Banner

Once the background piece is finished and pressed, place it on the **cutting board.** Line up the sides of the banner parallel to the grid lines. Secure the corners with pins stuck vertically into the cutting board. The design pieces are laid out and pinned in place the same way. When using Stitch Witchery or if sewing the pieces, stick the pins through the material so it will hold when the banner is picked up and taken to the ironing board or sewing machine. Sweep a magnetic pin holder over the work area to gather up the inevitable dropped pins.

Use **yardsticks** for placing the design pieces and keeping lines and words parallel. Yardsticks can be pinned in place to keep them from shifting. If several pieces of the design overlap, pin and glue the bottom layer first.

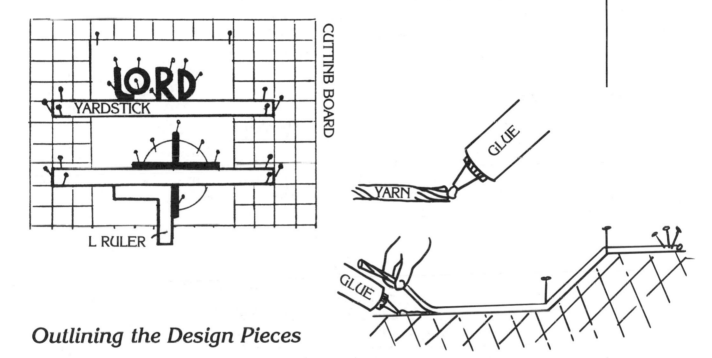

Outlining the Design Pieces

Each piece of the design is outlined with black rug yarn, permanent black felt-tip marker, or ¼" strips of soft, black felt. This emphatic definition of each color area creates the effect of stained glass. If a design piece is itself very dark or is set against a very dark background then omit the outlining as it will not be visible.

Rug, rather than regular, yarn is recommended because it provides a thicker line for separating the colors. If the yarn does not stick with glue then draw the outline with a black marker or use a glue gun. Two people may be needed to handle the glue gun and the yarn together.

☐ YARN

A dab of thick glue will keep the cut yarn ends from raveling. Stick two or three pins at various angles to hold the end of the yarn in place on the banner until the glue dries. Lay the yarn just over the top of the raw edges of the design or next to the edges when using nonraveling materials such as felt. When outlining corners use vertical pins to hold the yarn in position until the glue dries.

23

For long straight lines run a line of glue next to the edge of the yardstick. Then place the yarn down so it lies straight along the ruler. (If necessary iron wrinkles out of the yarn before beginning). To free both hands, pin the yardstick in place before gluing.

☐ FELT-TIP MARKER

A permanent black felt-tip marker may be used for the outline instead of yarn. Use the broader side (¼″) of the pen's nib. **Allow the black permanent ink to dry thoroughly before touching it or applying another color next to it.** Practice using a marker on a scrap to learn how to avoid making ink blobs which form when the pen is held too long in one spot on the fabric.

☐ FELT STRIPS

Narrow black felt strips may also be used in place of the black rug yarn. Place soft felt (the kind that can be gently stretched) on a plastic cutting board. Align a metal yardstick so ¼″ width strips can be cut with a rotary cutter. Curves can be formed by gently stretching the strip on the edge opposite to the curve. Wider strips cut this way can be used for other straight design pieces (e.g., the bars of a cross).

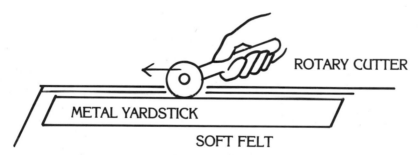

Tracing and Handling Letters

☐ PATTERNS

Letters may be glued, fused, or taped to the banner. The two most efficient methods for tracing letters involve polycoated freezer wrap paper:

1. Trace the letters onto the freezer paper (coated side down). Lay the traced sheet (coated side down) onto the right side of the fabric and press with a dry, medium iron. The heat will make the paper adhere to the fabric. Use lower heat and less pressing time for felt. Do a test piece first. Cut out the letters. Peel off the paper patterns. (These same paper patterns may be used repeatedly until the polycoating no longer bonds to fabric.) The fabric letters are ready to be glued or taped in place.

2. Xerox the alphabet pattern pages from this book. With rubber cement glue the xerox copies to the paper side of the freezer wrap allowing several

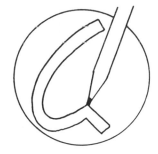

minutes to dry. Cut out the desired letters and continue as for method 1. These letter patterns may be reused although the letters are stiffer and will pop off the fabric more easily. If this is a problem then cut out the letters while the fabric is still warm.

Letter patterns can also, more simply, be cut directly from the xerox copies and pinned to the fabric for cutting. Or, for stability, they can be glued with rubber cement to file folders, cut, and used to trace around.

To save time make several sets of alphabet patterns to put aside until needed. In separate, labeled ziplock bags store (a) fusible freezer paper patterns, (b) patterns which are not fusible but can be pinned to the fabric for cutting, and (c) xerox-cemented patterns (not fusible) which can be outlined with a pencil or chalk pencil on fabric or (reversed on) Wonder-Under.

No matter how they are made, **precisely cut letters are essential for a finished look.**

☐ DRAWN LETTERS

Select Linear Alphabet B for drawing the letters on the banner with a marker. Use a ruler to make straight lines. Beware of ink collecting on the ruler's edge and fingers which can leave unwanted smears and prints on the fabric. For ease in marking the curves of letters prepare templates from plastic lids as follows:

1. Trace the curved letter on the pattern material (A).

2. With scissors or an X-acto knife cut the plastic template by following the outline of the letter (B). If unsure as to which side of the letter to cut do a sample with paper first.

3. Place the template in position on the banner and mark along the edge of the template where needed (C). Always use the broad side of the marker so the letter line is as wide as possible. Note how the letters *P* and *R* can be made like the *B* (D). Cut out the inner circle line on the letter *O* pattern for tracing with the marker.

☐ CAREFUL PLACEMENT

Use the cutting board's grid as a guide for the yardstick in placing and gluing words precisely on the banner. Use a 48″ yardstick or long lattice stick for vertically positioning any design pieces or strips. The yardstick is useful in aligning the right or left margins for several rows of words. **Proofread the words on the banner before attaching, checking for spelling errors and reversed letters.**

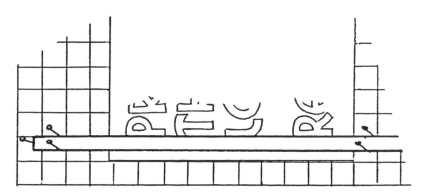

In this book each banner design indicates the approximate position of the words. Generally there is at least 1″ of space between the lines of words and also between the emblem and the letters. Note where the word(s) begin and end for each line on the graph; then **adjust the letters until all the words fit into the allotted space.**

☐ REMOVABLE LETTERS

It is possible to use a particular banner design for more than one occasion. The words can be changed if the letters are attached with **Scotch Double Stick Tape** or Scotch Double Stick Carpet Tape. Thus a single Lenten banner may be effectively used throughout the season simply by changing the captions. The mottos might be a series of sermon themes, Bible verses, or hymn titles. Store the unused letters (those with sticky tape on the back) on a sheet of wax paper. Use a gallon-size ziplock bag for storing the letters. Write the title of the banner and the words that are being stored in the bag on a self-sticking tag and attach it to the bag for easy identification. **Do not use polyester felt for removable letters.**

An alternate method for attaching removable letters is to press soft felt material (with no backing) firmly by hand onto a soft felt background (or one which has a toothy or fuzzy texture). This **flannelgraph** technique is appropriate for stationary banners placed in nonvulnerable locations only.

Gently remove felt letters from a soft felt background. The fibers will tend to pull out from the surface. If this happens pat the fibers back into place.

☐ LETTER STYLES

Almost all of the designs in this book use Circular Alphabet A. Alphabets B (Linear), C (Chalkboard), and D (Stencil), can be substituted for Alphabet A. Position the letter patterns on the full-size banner pattern to be sure the style chosen will fit comfortably in the space allowed. The width of some letters will vary slightly in the different alphabets. If the banner design has not been enlarged yet then position the letter patterns on the master grid or the cutting board in the same position as the design indicates. Alphabets E (Kindergarten) and F (Old German) have letters which are broader and need more space. Some banner designs have ample room; if not, then enlarge the width of the banner accordingly. **This planning of space should be done before purchasing the fabric.**

☐ CHANGING PROPORTIONS

When a banner is enlarged, the letters on it may become proportionately larger or smaller. To make patterns in the desired size use a variable-print copy machine. For example, Ban and Banner Set 66 could easily use 4″ letters on the side ban; or taller letters could be used for any words on the Christian Life or *JOY* Series (Banners 79–99) or a new banner design. The 3″ high letters can be enlarged to 4″ (33% increase), 5″ (67% increase), or 6″ (100% increase). Numbers from the print media may also be copy-machine altered for use on an anniversary banner (e.g., in the upper left-hand corner of Banner 76).

FORM AND CONTENT

Arranging the Design Elements

Both the *JOY* and the Christian Life Series (Banners 79–99) are based upon an open design which may be placed on backgrounds of varying size. Many other banners in this book have interchangeable emblems and optional wording. Still other totally new arrangements of design elements will be created by innovative banner makers. Essential to success in all of these cases is the establishment of a pleasing relationship between the words, the emblem, and the outer edges of the banner. Following are some general principles to apply to this purpose.

☐ RULES FOR SPACING AND ARRANGING LETTERS AND WORDS

Spacing between words is equal to the width of the letter *O*.

Leave the greatest distance between letters having parallel strokes.

Place a curved stroke a little closer to a straight line.

Two curved strokes are closer yet.

Two points are placed as close together as possible.

Some letters have variations in their shape or size. Select what is most appealing or fits best in a given area. Using the smaller *O*, for instance, is an attractive way to use less space.

If space is tight, letters may overlap or be altered.

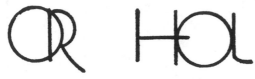

The space between words may be equal to an *H* or *N*.

Arrange columns of words so they line up on either the right or left side, or both.

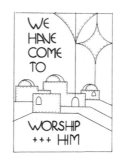

Group words as if inside an invisible oval, circle, rectangle, or square.

Do not stagger individual letters diagonally but have the whole word or group of words set on a diagonal line.

Arrange words clockwise from lower left to lower right.

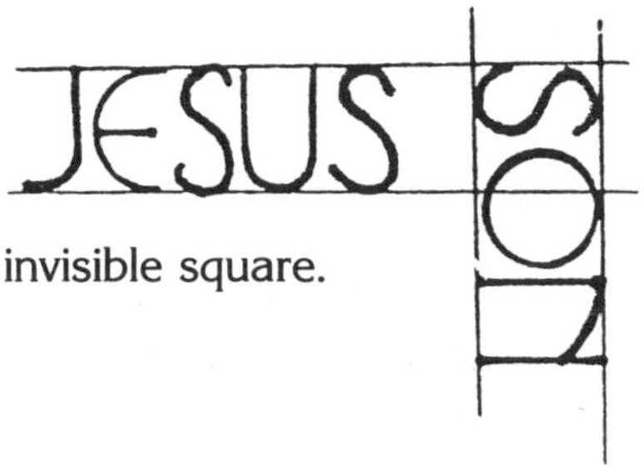

FOR THE + FORGIVENESS + OF SINS +

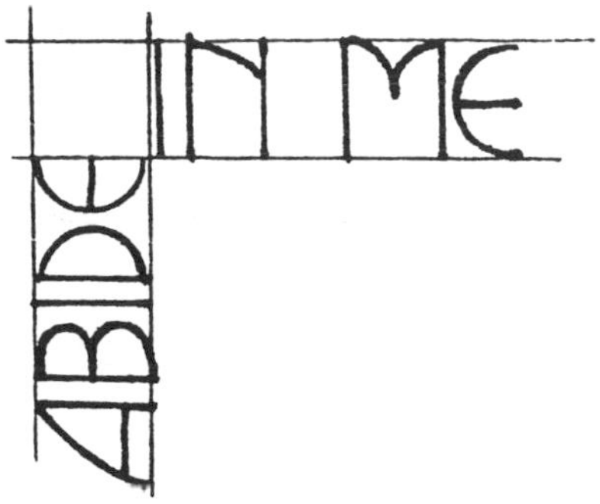

Words that meet at the corner should form an invisible square.

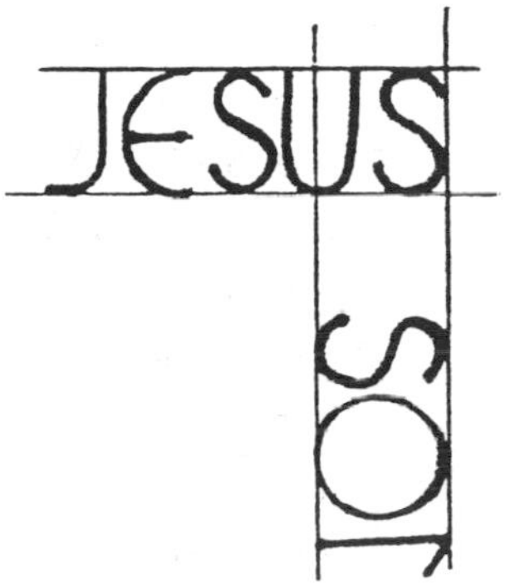

JESUS SON

ABIDE IN ME

JESUS SON

Long words in a short space may be separated into syllables. Arrange the syllables so they all line up evenly on the right side.

BLESS-
INGS

☐ RULES FOR SPACING BETWEEN THE WORDS/
EMBLEM AND THE BANNER'S BORDER/EDGE

For best results allow at least 3″ between the words/emblem and the out-side edge of the banner. This will vary according to the design used.

For a square banner allow equal space for the top and sides and more space at the bottom (A).

If a banner has a tall profile then the bottom space is largest and the top is wider than the sides (B).

If a banner has a wide profile then the bottom space is widest and the top space is smaller than the sides (C).

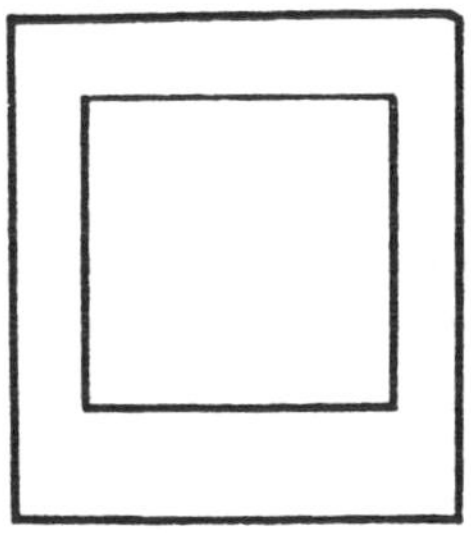

A

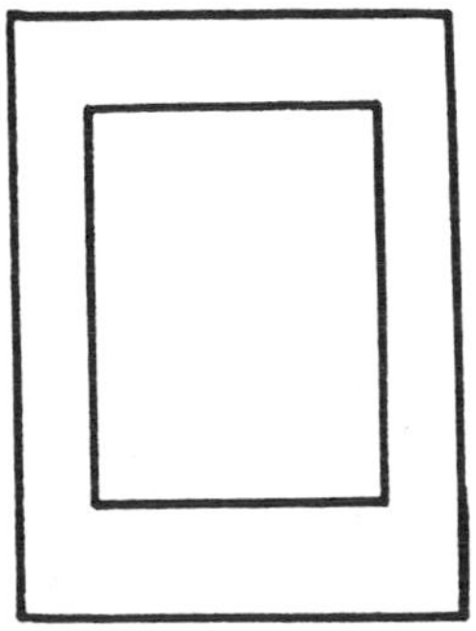

B

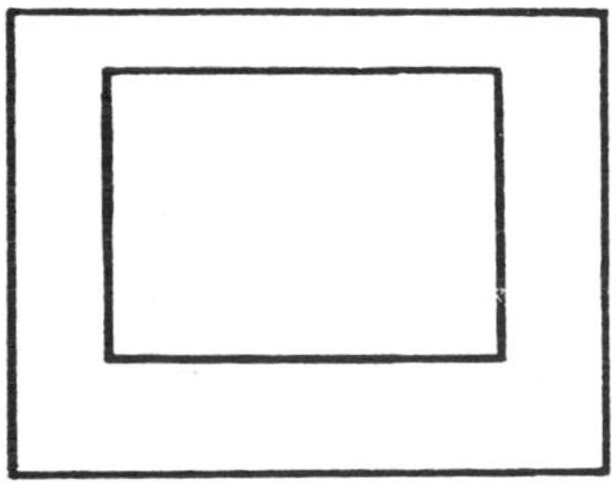

C

Checking the Composition

The composition and size of banners are intentionally flexible for the *JOY,*
Christian Life, and Wedding Series (Banners 70–99). If making one of
these or designing a new banner refer to the list of questions below to be
sure that the arrangement of color, shape, and content is eye-pleasing and
well balanced.

Composition Checklist

1. **What is the goal** (purpose, implied message, or theme) **of the
banner?**

2. **Does the banner communicate the goal(s)?** It should have an appropriate selection of word, color, and image.

3. **Is the banner arranged formally or informally?** Formal: the design on
one side is mirrored on the other (A). Informal: the banner has a balance
of content in different size areas (B).

4. **Is there a focal point?** This center of interest is created through (*a*)
color—high value and high density colors attract the eye first, (*b*) size—
large shapes are noticed first, and (*c*) placement—things in the center nat-
urally appear more important (C).

5. **Are the divisions** (the size of pieces or blocks of words and phrases,
color, and sequence) **logical, and is the total grouping of design pieces
interesting (D)?**

6. **Does the overall design have rhythm?** This is achieved by repetition
of shapes, color, and line (E).

A

B

C

D

E

30

7. Is movement within the design balanced? Vertical and horizontal lines look stable suggesting dignity and restraint (H). Diagonals suggest movement and action and should be limited in number and direction. Keep the design very simple to avoid clutter (E). Curved lines are active and work well moving into a composition to produce self-containment (F).

8. Is everything plainly marked for understanding? Symbols and/or words should be in logical order (G).

9. Does the arrangement of the words fit in with the total design? Keep the message as brief as possible while still maintaining clarity (H).

10. Is there adequate space between the emblem/words and the edge of the banner (unless the design extends to the edge)?

11. Is the number of colors limited? Use no more than three colors plus black and white.

12. Do the textures of the fabrics serve a special purpose? Wide wale corduroy, for instance, might be used to simulate wood texture, and satin might be a good choice for a special celebration banner.

13. Does it look overcrowded? The design should have restful negative areas and meaningful groupings of smaller elements. Details may be used to guide the eye from one area to the next (I).

14. Does it look overdecorated or simple and orderly? Avoid gaudy borders, unimportant items, or small unrelated pieces that are distracting (J).

15. Is everything neat in appearance? Ask this question continually while working on the banner. The edges should be precise, the seams invisible, and the fabric smooth.

16. Is there balance? The design should not be lopsided or too heavily concentrated in one area of the banner.

17. Does the design hang together? Unity is accomplished through use of related lines, color, shape, and content. Usually the eye will travel all over the banner starting and ending with the center of interest (I).

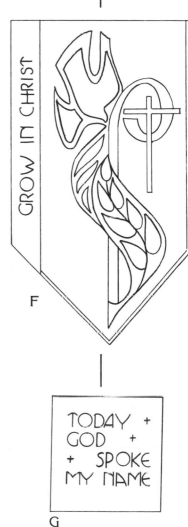

F

G

H

I

J

GROUP PROJECTS

Topstitching and Quilting Banners

Banners that are sewn and/or quilted take on an exciting new dimension. After liturgical service these banners can be put to practical use as blankets or quilts. The wedding, baptism, and confirmation banners and bans also make thoughtful gifts that may be used as wall hangings as well.

Some of the designs in this book lend themselves nicely to quilting. Consult other books or experienced quilters for technical instructions. Following are suggestions that specifically apply to quilting a banner:

1. If a banner is to be made into a quilt use only preshrunk, colorfast materials.

2. Allow 2″ to 3″ extra fabric for each side when buying the background fabric.

3. Use fusible interfacing (preshrink) or fusible web to line design pieces. They are then less likely to ravel and are more stable when stitched.

4. When quilting by machine use a Walking Foot. This attachment adjusts the tension on the top fabric to keep it from slipping forward when sewn. Write to Sewing Emporium, 1087 Third Avenue, Chula Vista, CA 92010 for price and information.

5. Yarn (preshrink), if used, is zigzagged on by machine; otherwise use a satin stitch to outline the design pieces.

6. Purchase fusible letters and iron them onto the fabric. Do a sample first.

7. Attach letters with Wonder-Under. They may not need satin stitch outlining to prevent raveling. Do a sample and fray test it by washing, drying, and handling the fabric. If the letter's edge survives the test then use this method.

8. Use quilted fabric such as the kind used for baby blankets and bathrobes as a substitute for the usual batting and cloth backing.

9. Stitch ¼″ away from the lines or edges of the words. If the letters are quite large then quilt around each letter. Quilt on both sides of a design line unless the space is too small.

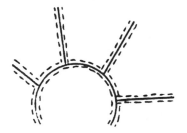   

10. Pin and quilt starting from the center of the banner and working outward.

11. After the banner is quilted measure and cut it to the required length and width. Bind the edges as a functional border for the banner.

Hanging the Banner

☐ CHOICE OF RODS

Determine the type of rod to be used for a banner before buying the background fabric. This information is necessary in order to estimate the fabric allowance for the top hem. The most inexpensive rod is a **lattice stick** which looks like an unmarked wooden yardstick. Carpenters may offer their leftover pieces for free. Check that the stick is thick enough to keep from sagging or bulging under the weight of the banner.

Flat wood is preferred for banners with designs that come within 2″ of or extend to the top edge. Otherwise any type of dowel including cut off broom handles, round sash cafe rods, or curtain rods may be used. **Wooden dowels of at least ½″ diameter** are strong enough to handle the weight of most banners without sagging. A large design such as Banner 25 would require a sturdy rod like a broom handle.

Cut **sticks and rods the same width as the banner** unless the cord is to be tied onto the end of the rod. To avoid having a banner slip around, stick two thumb tacks through the back of the fabric into the rod about an inch from each end. Color the last inch of each end with felt-tip marker to match the edge of the banner.

If the **rod extends beyond the sides of the banner,** the rod may be left its natural color or tinted to harmonize with the banner and the wall. Two nails on the wall on either side of the banner will support a rod without the use of a cord. Insert thumb tacks (for lightweight banners only), decorator nails, eye screws, upholstery tacks, or carpet tacks in each end of the stick leaving enough space for the cord to hook onto the shaft of the hardware. Cafe rods can be permanently adjusted to the proper length by taping them securely where the rods slide together. Only the sculptured end protrudes from the edge of the banner.

An alternate way to attach a banner to a lattice stick is illustrated in Banner A3. Position the tacks on the back as illustrated so that the stick and the banner hang well together. Or, use decorator nails or tacks on the front of the banner. Hang these lattice stick banners over two nails.

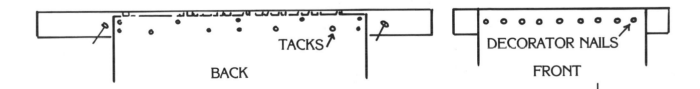

TACKS

BACK

DECORATOR NAILS

FRONT

Choose a **tie that harmonizes** with the banner and the wall such as macramé cord, yarn with a single crotched chain, heavy fishing line, a braid made from several strands of yarn, cords used as trim for sewing, decorator cords or tiebacks used with drapes, and metal or plastic chains. The length of the cord will be determined by how much it stretches. The following illustrations show how to attach cords to the ends of the stick or rod:

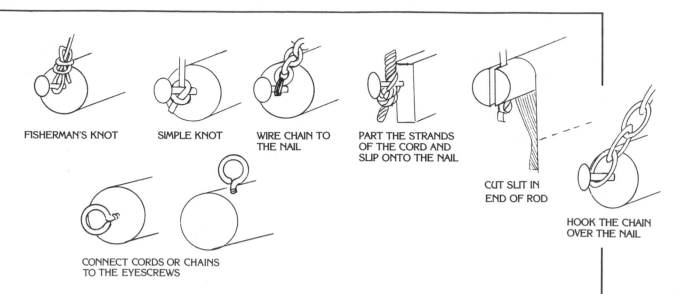

FISHERMAN'S KNOT

SIMPLE KNOT

WIRE CHAIN TO THE NAIL

PART THE STRANDS OF THE CORD AND SLIP ONTO THE NAIL

CUT SLIT IN END OF ROD

HOOK THE CHAIN OVER THE NAIL

CONNECT CORDS OR CHAINS TO THE EYESCREWS

☐ DISPLAYING THE BANNER

Consult the trustees of the church about where and how to hang the banners. Allow adequate space for the various size banners. **A banner should be seen by the congregation when it is seated.** If a wall cannot be used, have a wooden or metal freestanding pole made. Mr. Harold Ude designed and made the following wooden stand for St. John's Lutheran Church in Laurel, MT:

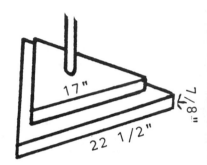

Slip the cord of the banner through the slit which has been cut in the top of the pole. The height of the pole is determined by where it is to be placed in the church and the length of the banners it is to hold.

Use a long pole with a hook to raise and lower the banners to nails or hooks already on the wall.

Storing Banners

Attach a self-sticking **label** to the back of each banner in an accessible-when-stored place. Include the following information on each:

1. the title and number of the banner

2. the quotation on the banner, or its theme (e.g., missions)

3. the name of the person(s) who made the banner

4. the date the banner was made

ADVENT CANDLES 17

WATCH PREPARE REJOICE BEHOLD

by Emma Polack

11-20-81

For easy reference a looseleaf **notebook** should be filled systematically with entries including a photo or sketch, a duplicate label, and the banner's location. The entries may be grouped according to season or theme.

Banners may be stored in cabinets or closets, along walls, hung from the backs of doors, from rafters, in storage rooms, in attics, or even in church members' garages or basements. The following illustration shows various ways to store banners:

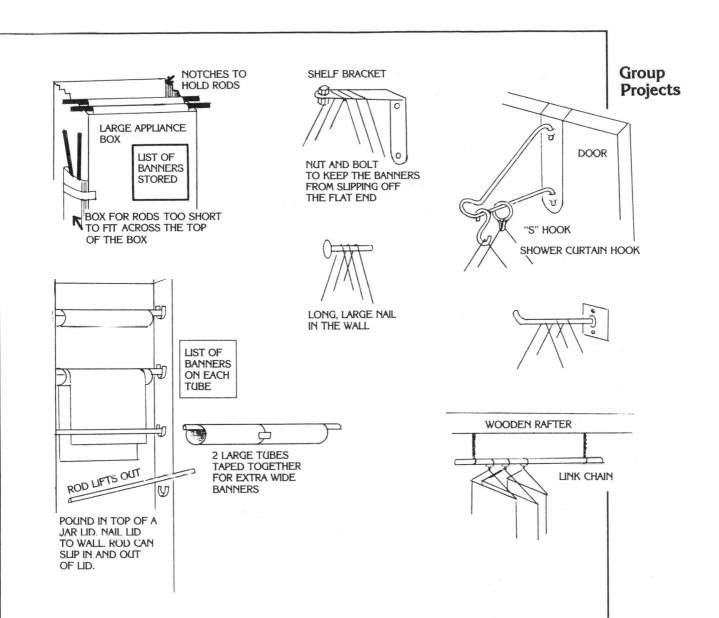

Group banners, if possible, by season (e.g., Lent) or theme (e.g., confirmation). Loosely tie a color-coded yarn or ribbon around the cords holding a particular group of banners. For example, tie a violet ribbon around the cords for the Lenten banners. Keep a master list and key for the color code in the looseleaf notebook. Hang banners so the designs face the wall. Protect them from dust by draping a cloth or plastic sheet over the banners. Be aware of the safety of small children when using plastic.

Banner Committee

The banner committee enlists people to make banners, sets up training workshops, arranges for banner workdays, solicits funds for the materials needed, keeps a looseleaf notebook with photos or design sketches and information on each banner, and provides for hanging and storing the banners. The church's altar guild is often placed in charge of such duties.

The banner design for a particular Sunday or celebration is selected by the banner committee in consultation with the minister. The pericopes (sets of Scripture readings recommended for each day in the liturgical calendar) should be read. *Banners for Worship* or a notebook of photos of banners already made are reviewed to find an appropriate design. A banner may be meaningfully displayed on more than one occasion especially if the committee composes a brief explanation of its symbolism to be printed in the church bulletin.

A **banner workshop** is an excellent way to encourage more people to become involved in making banners. Invite those who are interested or skilled in art, sewing, or crafts. Use *Banners for Worship* as a manual for training the beginners and introducing new techniques to the experienced. The workshop becomes a means of sharing the knowledge and sharpening the skills involved in assembling banners.

The banner committee in charge of the training workshop should decide which designs to use, invite people to attend, arrange to have all the required supplies and materials available, and (possibly) enlarge the designs to pattern size beforehand. Encourage **helpers** to attend also. These are people who do not wish to make a banner but are willing to iron, cut out letters and pieces of the design, or quilt. The workshop will not only produce a new set of banners but also train people in the special skills needed for making banners in the future.

Some people prefer to make banners on their own time at home. A **banner workday** can be arranged for those who wish to do their banners in a group setting. They can help each other when necessary and enjoy good fellowship in the process. Each person is responsible for bringing her/his own supplies and/or supplementing whatever the banner committee already has arranged. The items which are used communally such as ironing boards, irons, and large compasses can be brought by one or two people. It is best to assign one person to a banner and let that person choose her/his own helper (if needed). Making a banner is a step-by-step operation that often goes smoothly when accomplished by one independent worker. Quilting, on the other hand, is an activity in which a number of workers can productively cooperate.

Financing Banners

The banner committee arranges for financing the making of banners. By planning out the banners for a whole year and estimating their cost, a specific amount can be submitted to a church's budget committee. Some congregations set aside $300.00 to $400.00 annually for banners. A petty cash drawer of $50.00 is good to have for purchasing sale items. If this financial plan is not possible then post a sheet on which individuals and organizations may sign up to pay for the banners listed (include estimated cost),or accept donations. Usually a little enthusiasm and advertising in the bulletin or church newsletter generates funds. Most people actively appreciate the message and beauty that banners add to the worship service.

Some organizations and committees will offer to sponsor a banner made for a specific celebration such as a church anniversary, organ dedication, mortgage burning, or installation of a minister. An ornate banner may be commissioned for a wall space in the chancel, nave, narthex, or education wing. Many times the banner makers themselves will pay for the materials and consider it part of their contributions to the church. If a number of banners are done, though, the church or various organizations should offer to cover these expenses especially to **show appreciation for the banner makers** who are volunteering their services as well.

KEY TO THE DESIGNS

¼" in the book = 2" on the full-size design.

All numbers on the designs correspond to the numbered color chips in the **color key** on the back cover.

21/24: **First choice color** is 21 and second choice color is 24 for a designated area.

The **number next to a word** indicates its color. When all the words in a given motto are the same color, the number will be written only once.

A **large design area may be divided into smaller parts.** If only one of them is given a number, then the entire area should be the same color.

Only one star or cross of several on a banner will be assigned a color number. Color all the others the same.

¼", ⅜", or ⅝": designates **the width of a design line.**

————: indicates **shade lines** (solid lines made on the banner with a colored marker).

W: white.

B: black.

G: metallic gold.

S: metallic silver.

Experiment with **metallic trims** to see whether they are striking enough to enhance the design.

All **internal design lines are made with black rug yarn or ¼" soft, black felt strips** unless they separate a color from a black or very dark area. There is no need to outline a ribbon or band applied to the edges.

A1, A2, A3, etc.: illustrate alternate combinations of design elements which produce new banners.

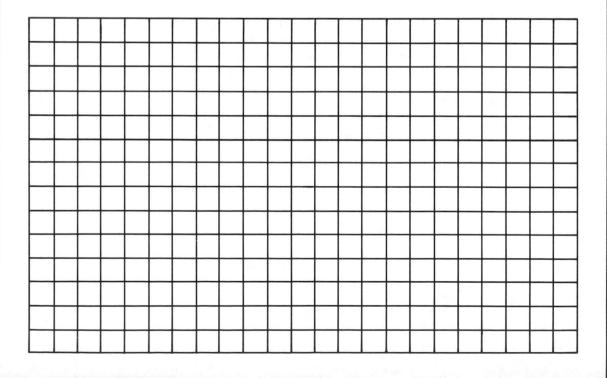

BANNERS FOR THE CHURCH YEAR

1,2,3,4 ADVENT SET OF FOUR BANNERS

5,6,7,8 ADVENT SET OF FOUR BANNERS

9,10,11,12 ADVENT SET OF FOUR BANNERS

13,14,15,16 ADVENT SET OF FOUR BANNERS

17 ADVENT CANDLES

18 CHRISTMAS LAMB

19 CHRISTMAS ANGEL

20 CHRISTMAS JOY

21,22,23 MATCHING BANNER SETS
*   FOR CHRISTMAS, LENT, AND EASTER*

24 COORDINATED CHRISTMAS ANGEL

25 COORDINATED EASTER ANGEL

26 NEW YEAR'S BLESSING

27 EPIPHANY CROWN

28 EPIPHANY TOWN

29 ASH WEDNESDAY CROSS

30 LENT LAMB

31 LENT/GOOD FRIDAY GOLGOTHA

32 PALM SUNDAY HOSANNA

33 PALM SUNDAY/CONFIRMATION PALM BRANCH

34 MAUNDY THURSDAY/
*   COMMUNION BREAD AND WINE (a)*

35 MAUNDY THURSDAY/
*   COMMUNION BREAD AND WINE (b)*

36 EASTER SUNRISE

37 EASTER LILY

38 EASTER MESSAGE

39 EASTER LILIES

40(a) EASTER BUTTERFLY
*   (b) EASTER BUTTERFLY ALTERNATE*

41 EASTER RESURRECTED CHRIST

42 PENTECOST ENTERING DOVE

43 PENTECOST GIFTS

44 TRINITY SUNDAY HAND IN DOVE

45 TRINITY SUNDAY GEOMETRY

PRINCE OF PEACE

JESUS, SON OF GOD

COUNSELOR
WONDERFUL

EMMANUEL
EMMANUEL

ALTERNATE COLORS

MAY BE USED AS PARAMENTS:

LECTERN—BANNER 1
PULPIT—BANNER 2
ALTAR, LEFT—BANNER 3
ALTAR, RIGHT—BANNER 4

1,2,3,4 ADVENT SET OF FOUR BANNERS

PRINCE OF PEACE

B | W

2

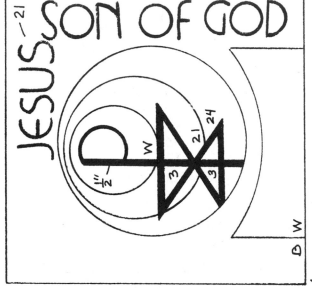

JESUS, SON OF GOD

B | W

4

COUNSELOR
WONDERFUL

W | B

1

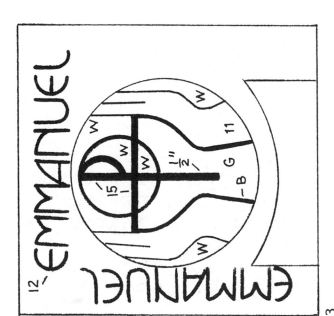

EMMANUEL
EMMANUEL

3

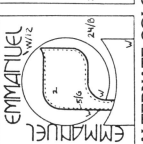
PRINCE OF PEACE
w/16

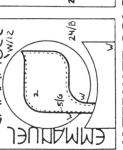
JESUS SON OF GOD
w/21

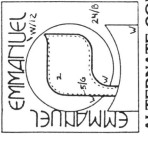
COUNSELOR
w/2
WONDERFUL

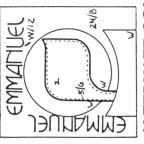
EMMANUEL
w/12
EMMANUEL

ALTERNATE COLORS

REJOICE BEHOLD

PREPARE
WATCH
w/1
w 24

USE AS ALTAR PARAMENTS

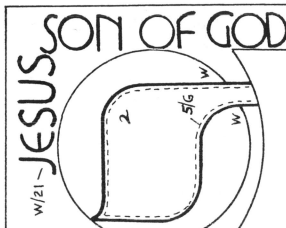

ALTERNATE EMBLEMS

5,6,7,8 ADVENT SET OF FOUR BANNERS

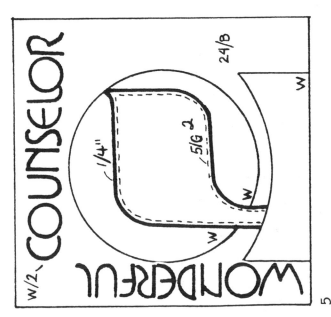

PRINCE OF PEACE
w/16
2 5/G w w
24/B
6

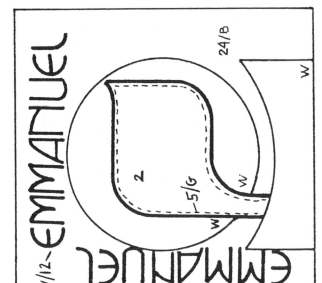

JESUS SON OF GOD
w/21
2 5/G w w
24/B
8

COUNSELOR
w/2
WONDERFUL
1/4" 5/G 2 w w
24/B
5

EMMANUEL
w/12
EMMANUEL
2 5/G w w
24/B
7

SHADE LINES ARE OPTIONAL

41

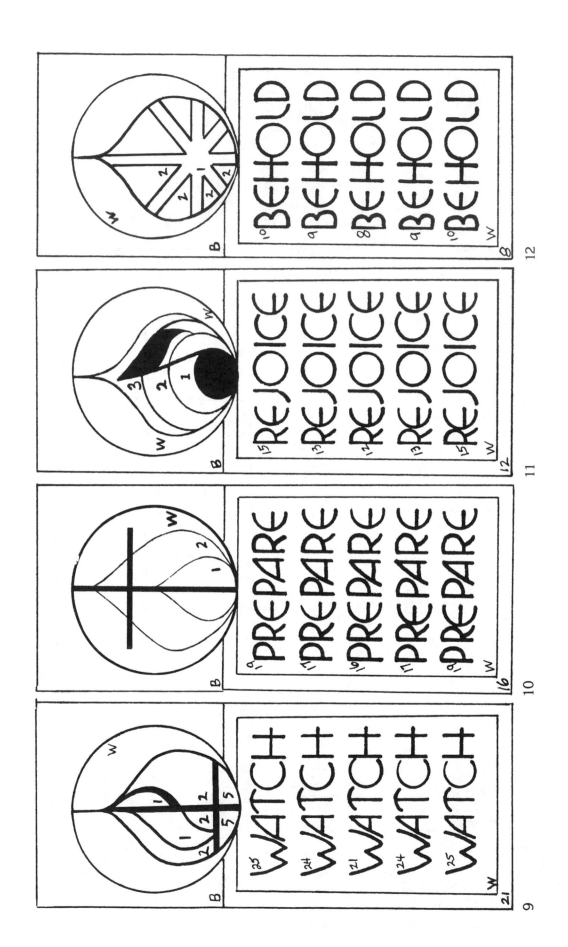

9,10,11,12 ADVENT SET OF FOUR BANNERS

42

13, 14, 15, 16 ADVENT SET OF FOUR BANNERS

PRINCE OF PEACE
LAMB OF GOD

18 CHRISTMAS LAMB

BEHOLD
REJOICE
PREPARE
WATCH

17 ADVENT CANDLES

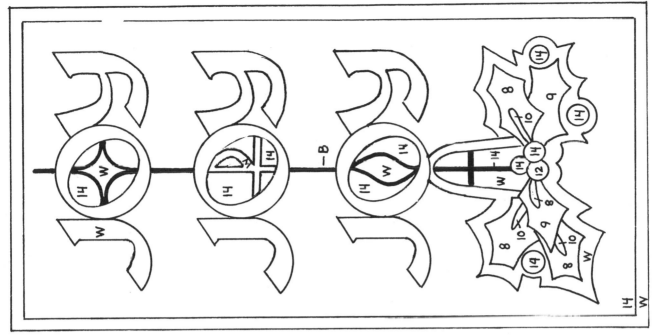

20 CHRISTMAS JOY

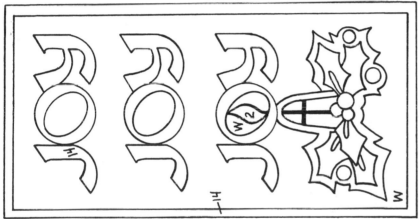

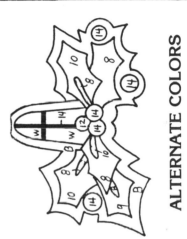

ALTERNATE COLORS

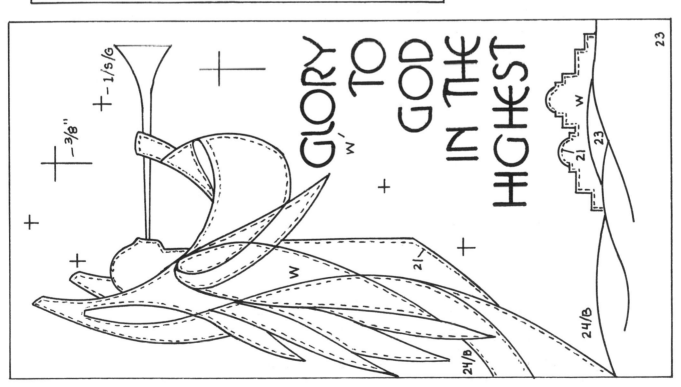

GLORY
TO
GOD
IN THE
HIGHEST

19 CHRISTMAS ANGEL

45

HE LIVES

HE DIED

HE CAME

23 Easter: *He Lives*

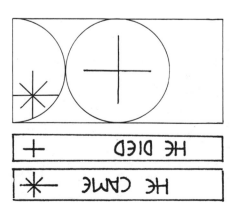

21 Christmas: *He Came*

HE CAME

22 Lent: *He Died*

HE DIED

HE CAME

46

peace on earth

Good will to men

ALTERNATE COMBINATION FOR CHRISTMAS:

ALTAR-LEFT, BANNER 24 WITH THE WORDS

GOOD NEWS OF GREAT JOY

GLORY TO GOD

he is not here †
he has risen †

25 COORDINATED EASTER ANGEL

ALTERNATE CHRISTMAS/EASTER COMBINATION:

ALTAR-RIGHT, BANNER 25 WITH THE WORDS

PEACE ON EARTH

GOOD WILL TO MEN

48

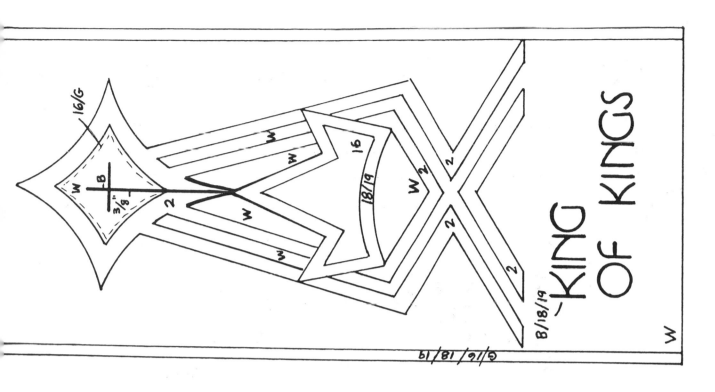

27 EPIPHANY CROWN

26 NEW YEAR'S BLESSING

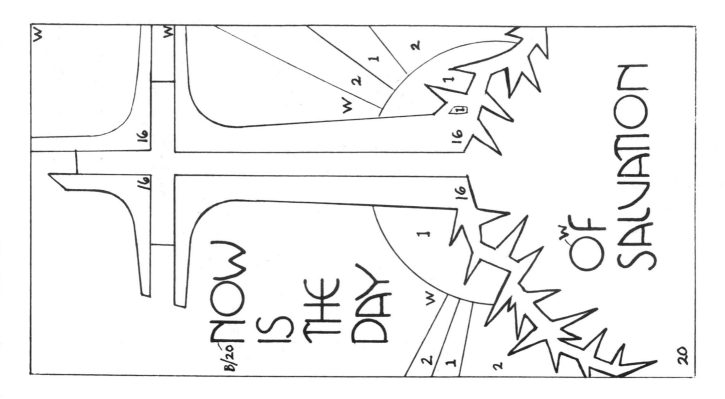

B/26 NOW IS THE DAY OF SALVATION

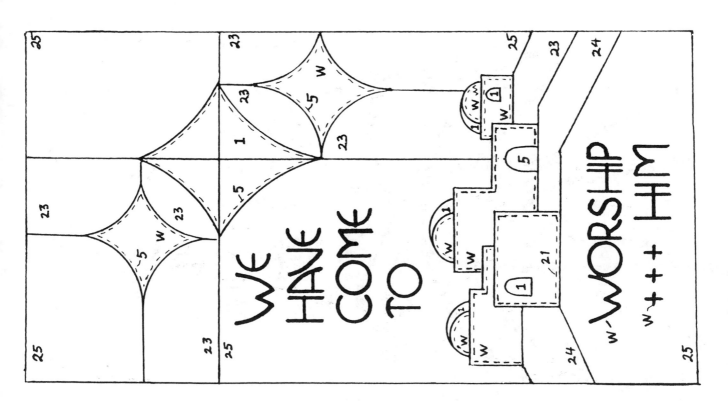

WE HAVE COME TO WORSHIP HIM

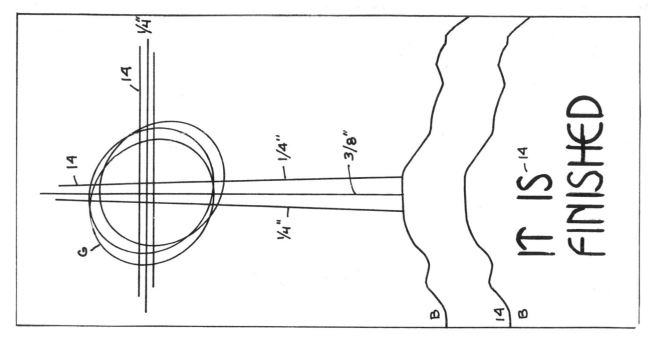

IT IS FINISHED

31:ALTERNATE CROWN

Drape and loop ¼" wide, gold ribbon into three intertwining circles. Allow the center of the loop to gap ½" or less from the surface of the banner. Use dots of glue to hold the loops in position.

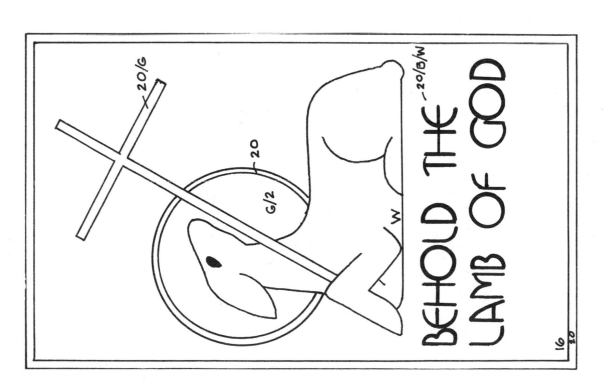

BEHOLD THE LAMB OF GOD

30 LENT LAMB

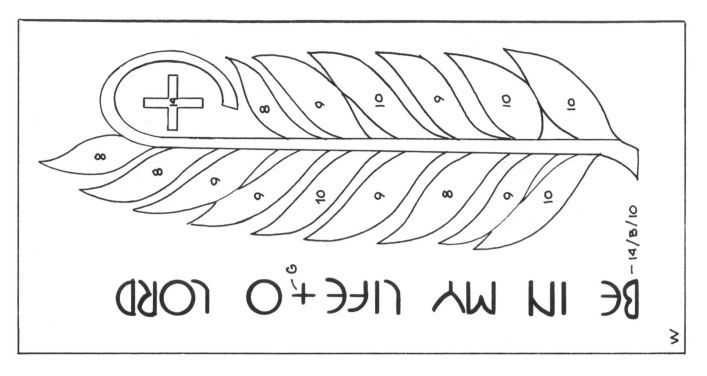

BE IN MY LIFE O + LORD

— 14/B/10

33 PALM SUNDAY/CONFIRMATION PALM BRANCH

hosanna hosanna

HOSANNA HOSANNA

HOSANNA IN THE HIGHEST

ALTERNATE WORDING

HOSANNA

MAY BE USED AS AN ALTAR PARAMENT

32 PALM SUNDAY *HOSANNA*

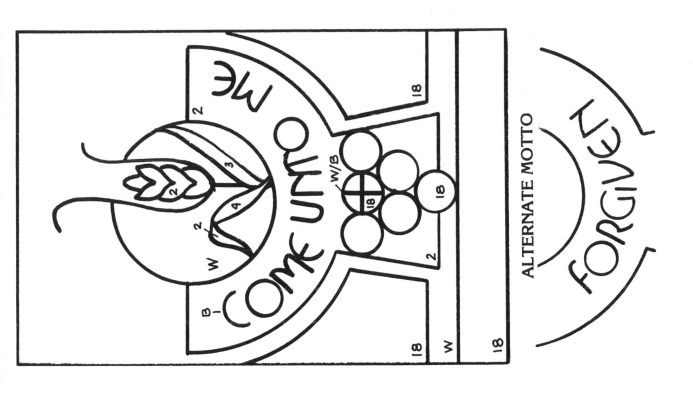

ALTERNATE MOTTO

FORGIVEN

**35 MAUNDY THURSDAY/
COMMUNION BREAD AND WINE (b)**

MAY BE USED AS AN ALTAR PARAMENT

**34 MAUNDY THURSDAY/
COMMUNION BREAD AND WINE (a)**

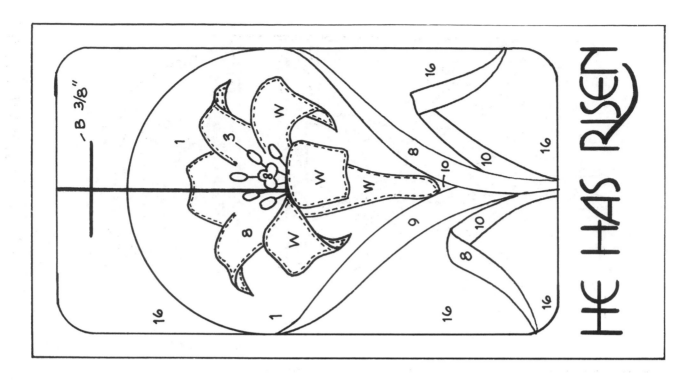

He has risen

37 EASTER LILY

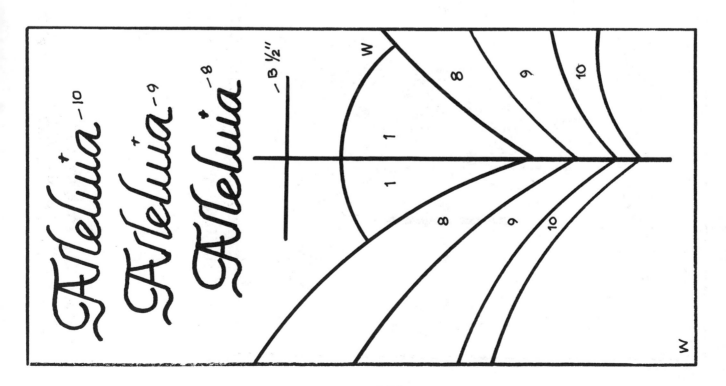

36 EASTER SUNRISE

39 EASTER LILIES

MAY BE USED AS AN ALTAR PARAMENT

38 EASTER MESSAGE

LOVE
JOY
PEACE
PATIENCE
KINDNESS
GOODNESS
FAITHFULNESS
GENTLENESS
SELF-CONTROL

43 PENTECOST GIFTS

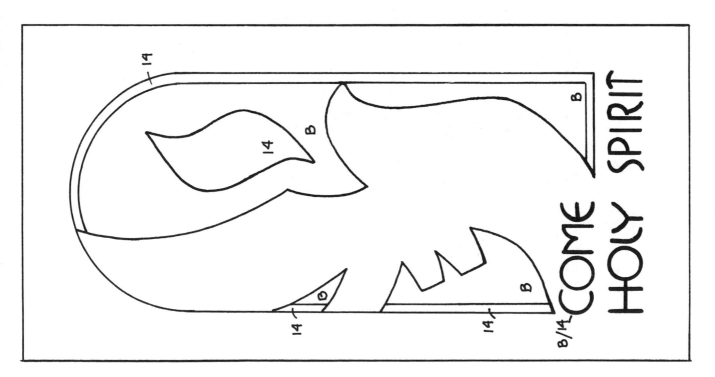

COME HOLY SPIRIT

42 PENTECOST ENTERING DOVE

MAY BE USED AS AN ALTAR PARAMENT

45 TRINITY SUNDAY GEOMETRY

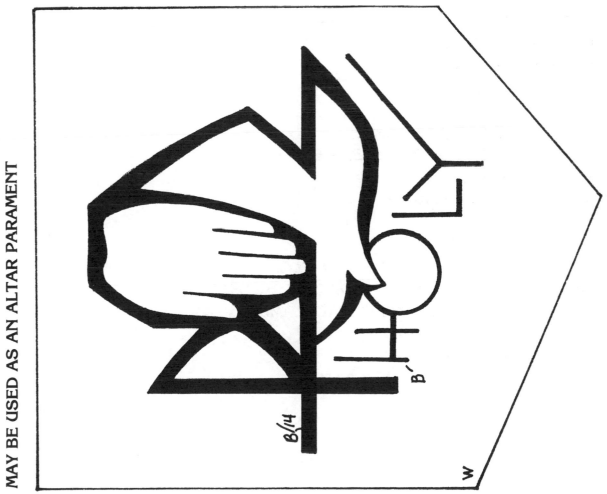

44 TRINITY SUNDAY HAND IN DOVE

BANNERS FOR SPECIFIC OCCASIONS

47 THANKSGIVING SEASONS

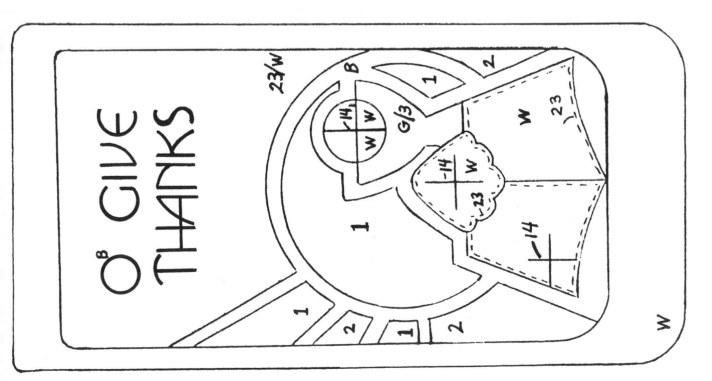

46 THANKSGIVING RADIANCE

BAPTIZED INTO CHRIST

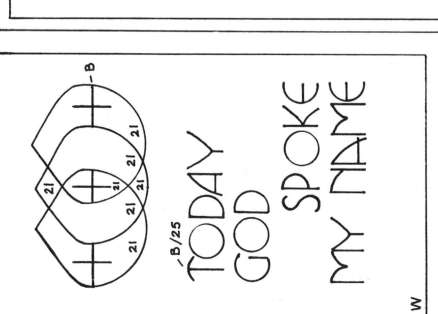

THANK YOU + GOD FOR + KENDRA

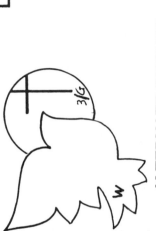

TODAY GOD SPOKE MY NAME

50 BAPTISM DOVE

ALTERNATE EMBLEM
49 BAPTISM GIFT

48 BAPTISM WATER DROPS

52 BAPTISM CANDLE

ALTERNATE MOTTOS

CHILD †
OF GOD †
DIANNA ÷

÷ † ABIDE
IN CHRIST
ALWAYS †

THE GIFT
OF FAITH †

GROW † † †
IN CHRIST

† † TODAY
GOD SPOKE
MY NAME †

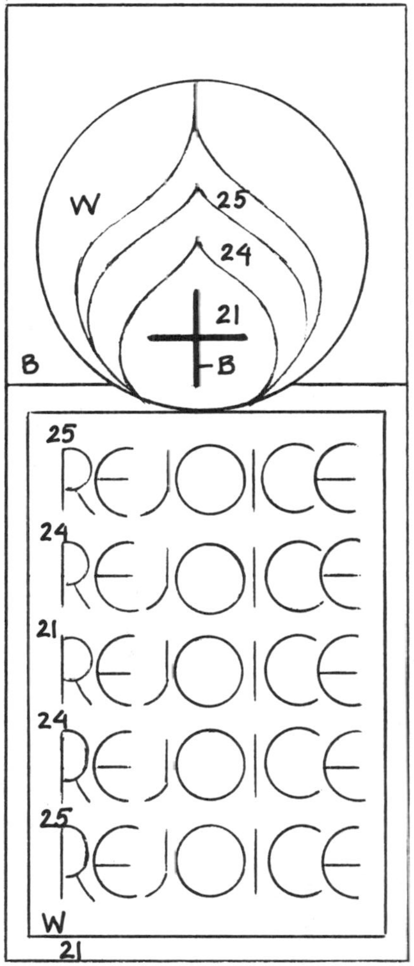

51 BAPTISM SHELL

REJOICE

KENNETH 60

KELLY 59

GROW IN CHRIST 58

TODAY GOD SPOKE MY NAME 57

THANK YOU GOD FOR ERIC 56

JOEL 55

CHILD OF GOD NICKIE LYNN 54

THE GIFT OF FAITH 53

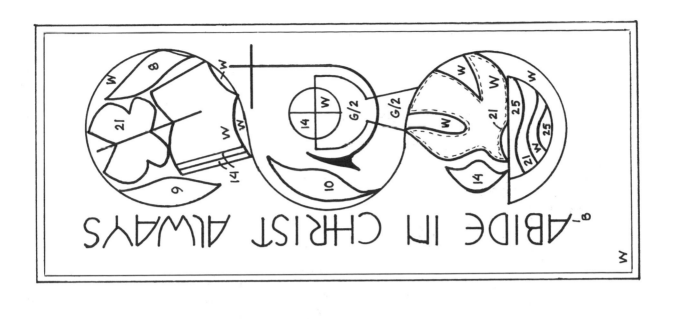

63 CONFIRMATION VINE

**62 CONFIRMATION
CROSS-CROOK**

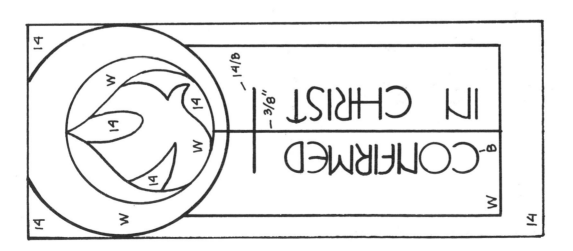

61 CONFIRMATION CANDLE

BE FAITHFUL

W /16

ALTERNATE BANNERS:

ADD LENGTH TO EITHER BANNER AND ARTISTICALLY ARRANGE THE NAMES OF THE CONFIRMANDS BELOW THE EMBLEM

65 CONFIRMATION CROWN

A2

BE FAITHFUL

LINDA JUNE +
JASON BOB
KATHY JUDY
DON LAURIE
+ JONATHON

GROW IN CHRIST

JENNIFER
+EDWARD
LUKE TOM
BETTY ++
+ GLORIA
JEANETTE

A1

64 CONFIRMATION CIRCLE

GROW IN CHRIST

W

14/B

WIDEN THE BAN AND ENLARGE THE LETTERS PROPORTIONATELY

66 CONFIRMATION BAN AND BANNER SET

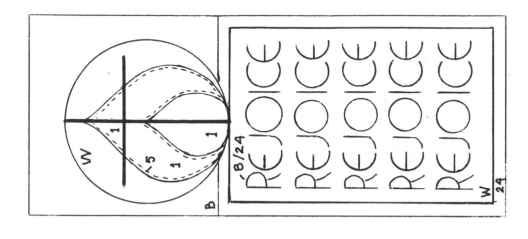

CHRIST WITH US

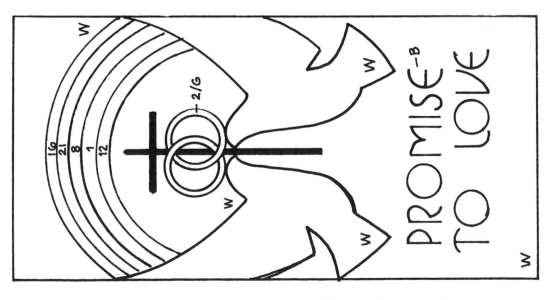

PROMISE TO LOVE

67 WEDDING RAINBOW   68 WEDDING HEARTS   69 WEDDING CANDLE

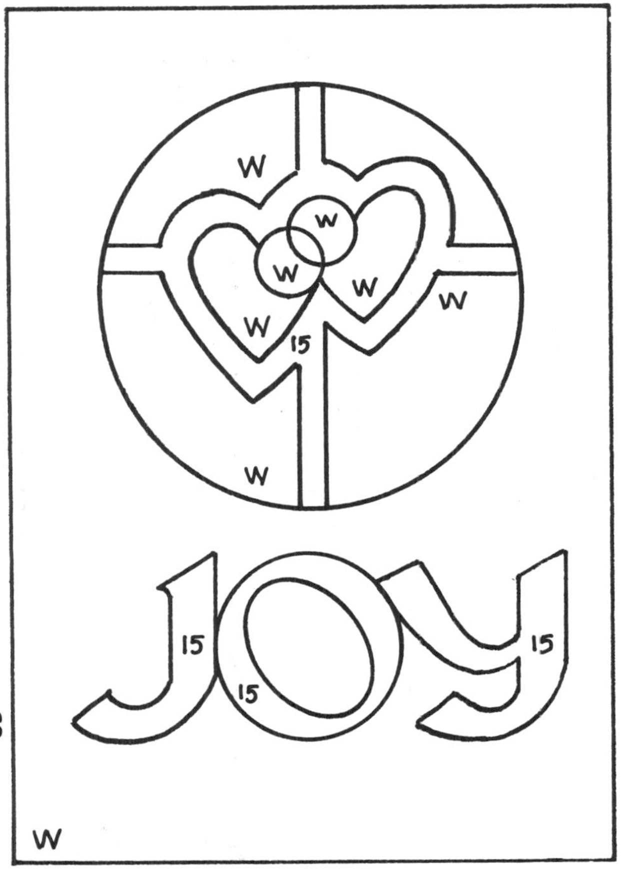
W
W
W
W
W
W
15
W
JOY
15
15
15
W

70 HEARTS BANNER

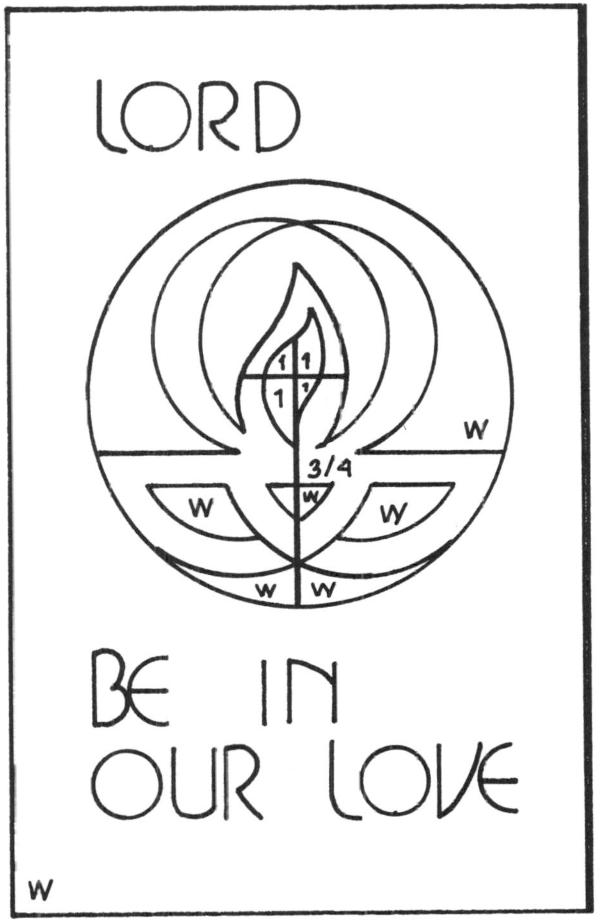
LORD
1 1
1 1
W
3/4
W
W
W
W W
BE IN
OUR LOVE
W

71 FLAMES BANNER

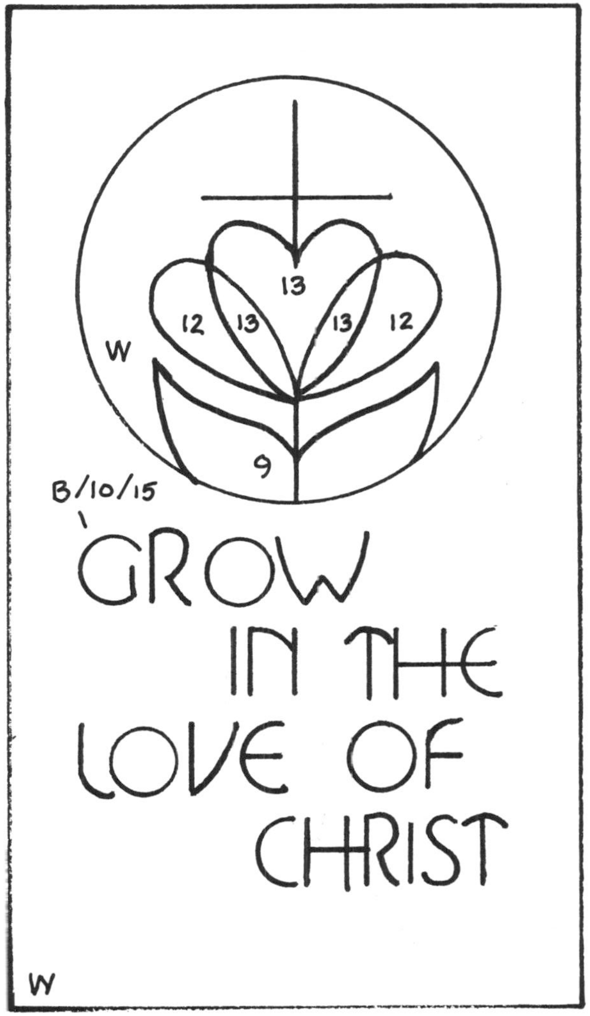
13
12 13 13 12
W
9
B/10/15
GROW
IN THE
LOVE OF
CHRIST
W

72 FLOWER BANNER

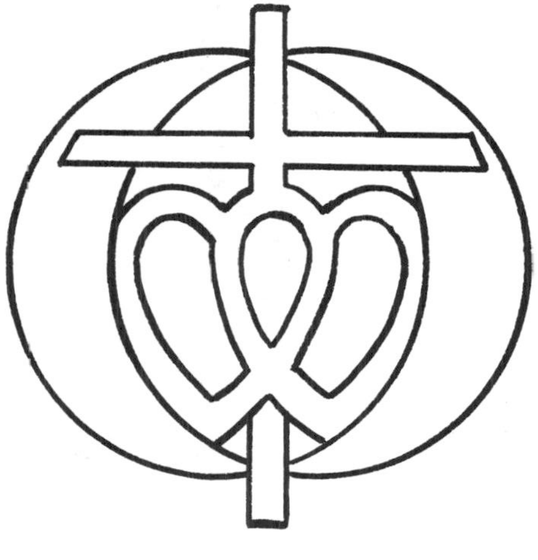

73 HEART-CROSS EMBLEM

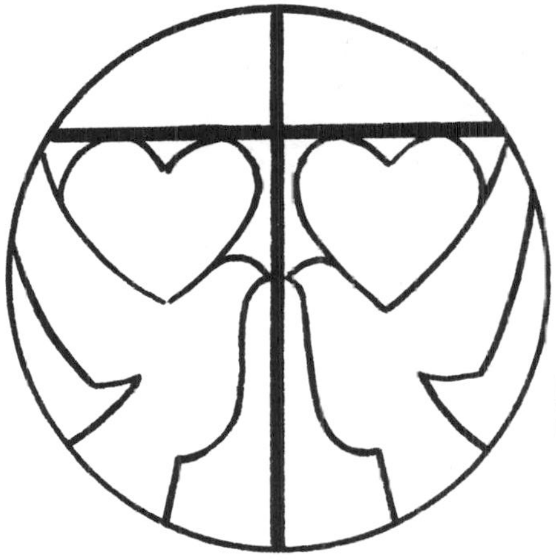

74 DOVES EMBLEM

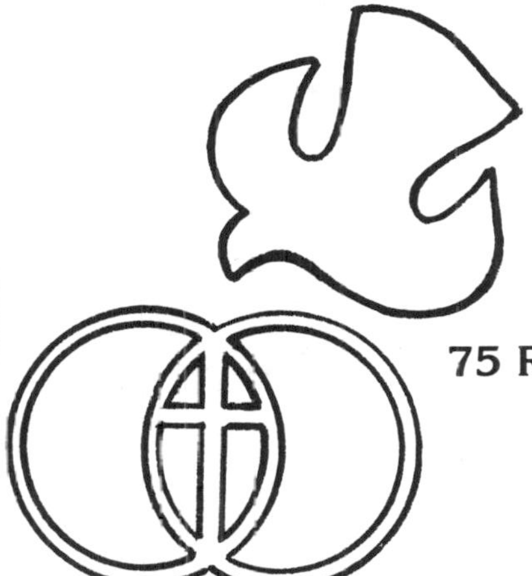

75 RINGS EMBLEM

70–75 WEDDING SERIES

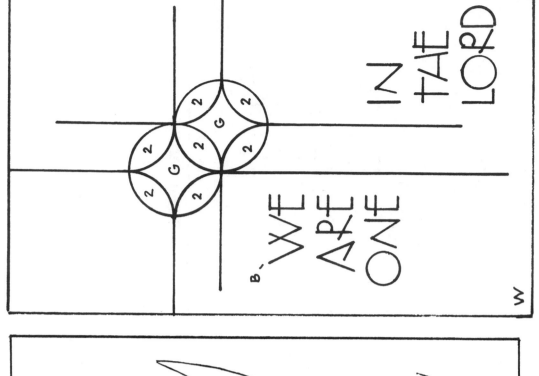

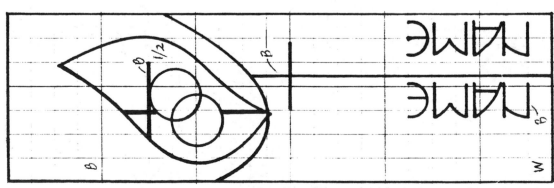

76 WEDDING CANDLE
WITH NAMES

77 WEDDING SEAGULLS
AND SUNSHINE

78 WEDDING BANDS

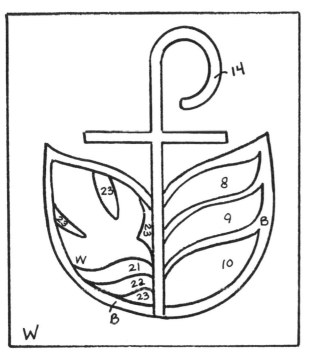

79 BAPTISM

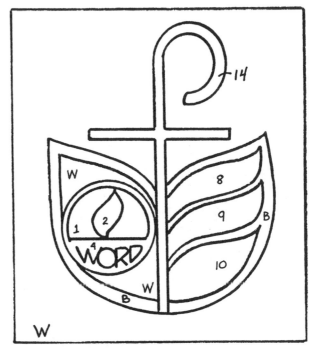

80 CHRISTIAN EDUCATION

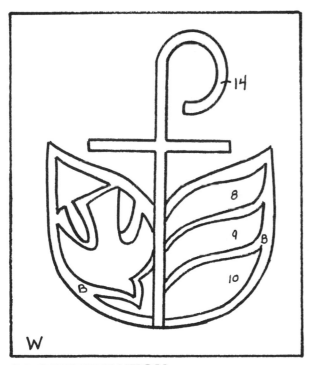

81 CONFIRMATION

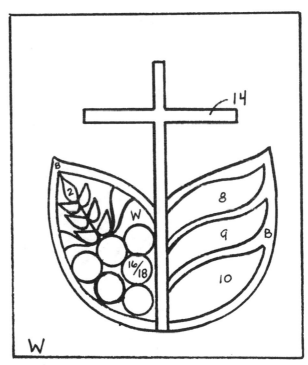

82 COMMUNION

MAY BE USED AS PARAMENTS

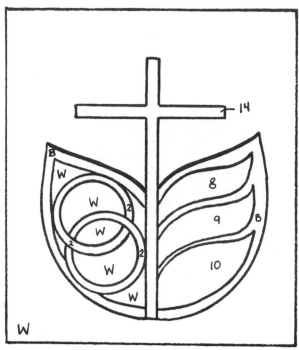

83 WEDDING

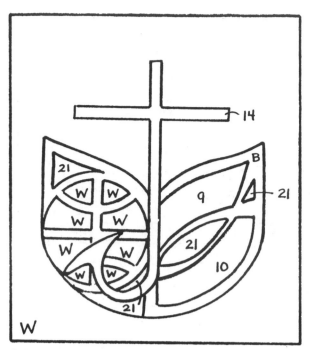

84 MISSIONS

85 DEATH/RESURRECTION

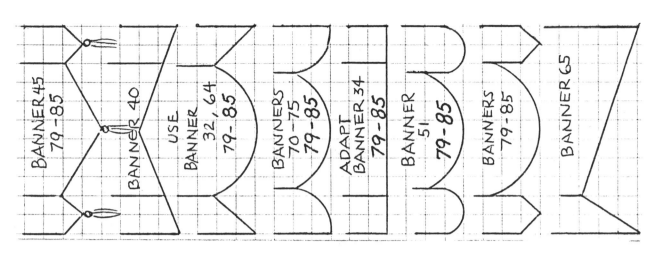

ALTERNATE BANNER BASES USING
SEPARATE SIDE BANS OF
CONTRASTING OR HARMONIZING COLOR:
WORDS MAY BE PUT ON
THE SIDE BANS

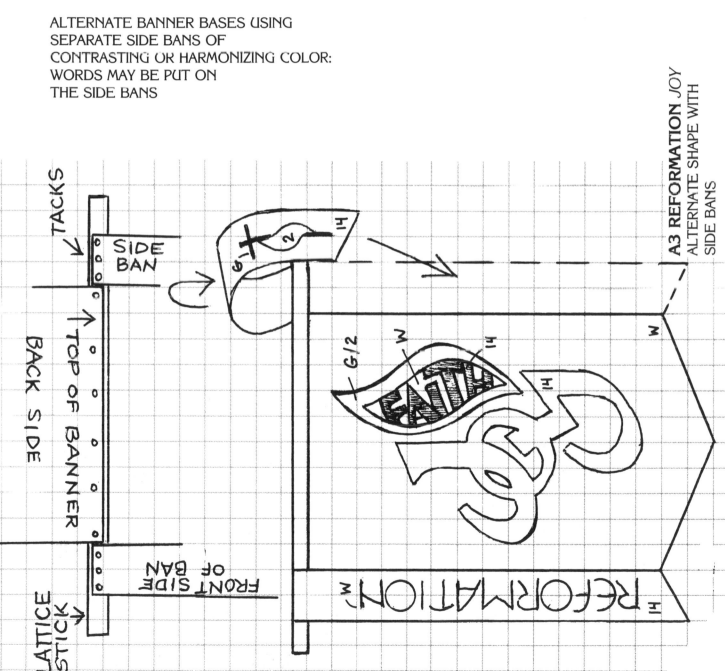

73

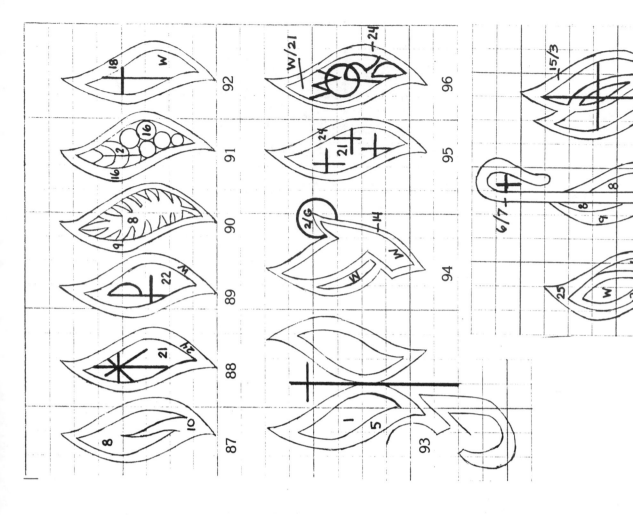

86 PENTECOST/LIGHT OF THE WORLD

87 GROWTH
88 LIGHT/CHRISTMAS/EPIPHANY
89 CHI-RHO/CHRISTMAS
90 PALM SUNDAY
91 COMMUNION/MAUNDY THURSDAY
92 LENT
93 EASTER
94 HOLY SPIRIT/BAPTISM/
CONFIRMATION/PENTECOST
95 BAPTISM
96 WORD
97 FISH/SAVIOR/MISSIONS
98 GOOD SHEPHERD/ORDINATION
99 WEDDING/ANNIVERSARY

MAY BE USED AS PARAMENTS

GIVE GOD THE GLORY

LET YOUR LIGHT SHINE

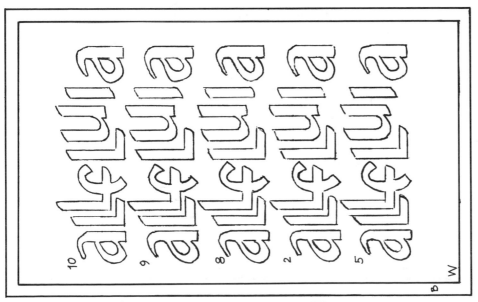

101 INSTALLATION OF CHURCH WORKER LAMP

100 ALLELUIA CHORUS

FEED MY LAMBS

FEED MY LAMBS
VIOLA
A5

LEONARD FEED MY SHEEP
A4

**ALTERNATE
PERSONALIZED BANNERS**

**103 INSTALLATION OF
CHURCH WORKER LAMB**

PREACH B/14 THE GOOD NEWS

TO ALL PEOPLE

B/14

14

14

14

3/2

W

W

3/2

14

14/G

**102 INSTALLATION/ORDINATION
FLOCK OF CROSSES**

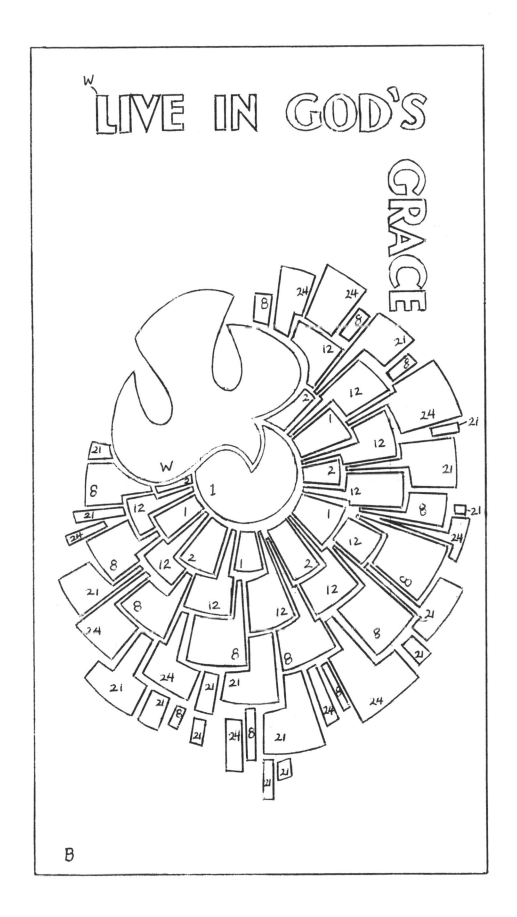

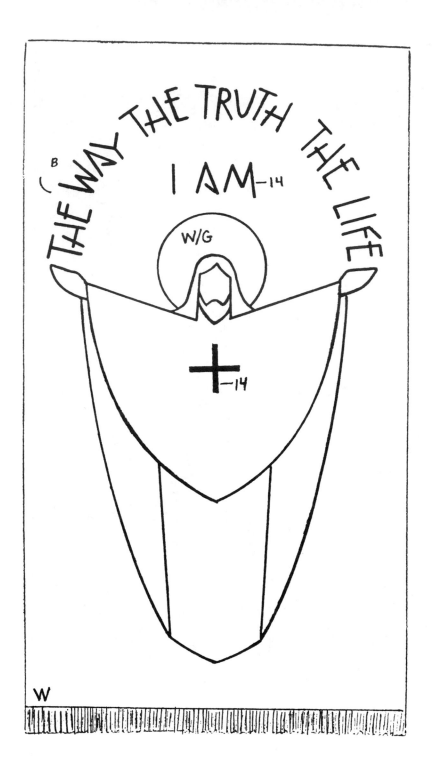

ALPHABET PATTERNS

A: CIRCULAR ALPHABET
B: LINEAR ALPHABET
C: CHALKBOARD ALPHABET
D: STENCIL ALPHABET
E: KINDERGARTEN ALPHABET
F: OLD GERMAN ALPHABET

A: CIRCULAR ALPHABET

C: CHALKBOARD ALPHABET

TOZI
NJED
BLVG

F: OLD GERMAN ALPHABET

92

k

Design Information

BANNERS FOR THE CHURCH YEAR

1, 2, 3, 4 Advent Set of Four Banners

Hang all four banners the first week of Advent or hang one banner each week beginning with Banner 1 for the first Sunday, Banner 2 for the second Sunday, etc.

One option for Banners 1–8 is to hang Banners 1, 6, 7, 8 the first week of Advent. The second week display Banners 1, 2, 7, 8; the third week have Banners 1, 2, 3, 8; and the fourth week hang Banners 1, 2, 3, 4. If this grouping is used then make the circle-designs of Banners 1–4 and the flame-halos of Banners 5–8 interchangeable for the backgrounds of Banners 1–4. This is done by using double stick tape to attach the emblems to the banners rather than gluing them onto the backgrounds permanently. Or make all eight banners and display as needed.

SYMBOLISM: Banners 1–4 use a white (purity) candle base with a circle (halo) above. The emblems take the place of the candle flame (Christ as the Light of the world) showing other attributes of Jesus. The black background is the darkness of sin that Christ illuminates.

Banner 1: The red cross brings to mind the Red Cross Organization that offers help throughout the world. Christ (hand) takes care of all of man's needs including the spiritual. Jesus gave His own life (cross) that all might have eternal life (circle).

Banner 2: The sign of peace (hand) is given in the Benediction. The crown is for the royal Christ.

Banner 3: Emmanuel means God with us. The Greek letters, Chi (X) and Rho (P), are the beginning of the word Christ. The Chi-Rho is superimposed on the circle (bread) and cup (wine) showing His presence in the elements of Communion.

Banner 4: The Chi-Rho forms the manger. Three circles represent the Triune God.

ALTERNATE USE: Communion—Banner 3; Christmas—Banners 1, 2, 3, 4.

5, 6, 7, 8 Advent Set of Four Banners

Hang all four banners the first week of Advent or one each week beginning with Banner 5.

SYMBOLISM: The four candles are lighted sequentially during the four Sundays in Advent. Christ is the Light of the world (flame). The words are epithets for the awaited Lord.

ALTERNATE USE: General—Words or phrases can be interchanged by using double stick tape. Choose key words or phrases from the pericopes of the three year lectionary, the sermons, or hymns (consult the minister). The following illustration is an example of how the banner's wording can be changed to make Christ its theme.

A6

For missions change the wording as illustrated below.

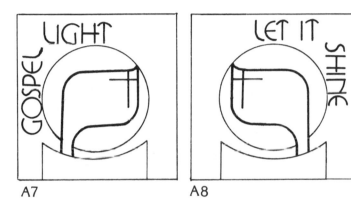

A7   A8

9, 10, 11, 12 Advent Set of Four Banners

SYMBOLISM FOR BANNERS 9–12: All banners show Christ as the Light of the world (candle). Each of the words chosen is central to the pericopes for the Sundays in Advent. The flame in Banner 9 has a Chi (X)-Rho (P), the first two letters in the Greek word for Christ, showing that the worshipers watch for His second coming. The flame in Banner 10 has a cross reminding the worshipers to prepare their hearts through repentence. The musical note in the flame of Banner 11 suggests one way of rejoicing on Jubilate Sunday (third Sunday of Advent). The cross/star flame of Banner 12 is symbolic of Christ, who was prophesied as the star that would come out of Jacob (Numbers 24:17).

ALTERNATE USE for Banner 11: Celebration—Use for a musical event, dedication of a new organ, etc. The wording may be changed to suit the occasion.

13, 14, 15, 16 Advent Set of Four Banners

Hang all four banners the first week of Advent or one banner per week beginning with Banner 13.

SYMBOLISM: The symbolism for the flames is the same as for Banners 9–12. Banner 15 features a horn calling to mind the joyful noise made by God's people. The mottos, key words or phrases from Advent hymns, may be changed as desired. Consult the minister.

ALTERNATE WORDING: The following illustrates how the words from Banners 1–4 and 9–12 can be used on the candle base.

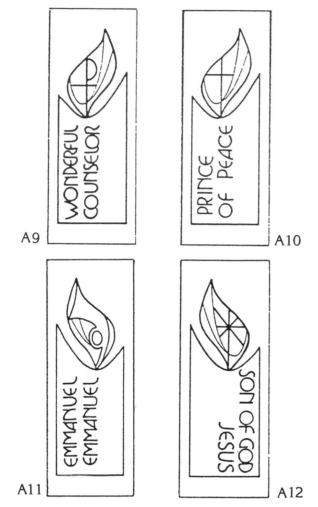

A9

A10

A11

A12

Use the same colors for the words as indicated for Banners 9–12.

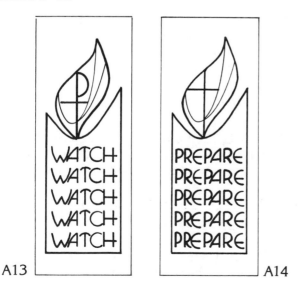

A13

A14

A15

A16

ALTERNATE COLOR SCHEME: 1. The candle base is white with a blue, violet (match the color of the paraments), or black background. If the background is violet then use magenta (17) or hot pink (12) for the banner being used for the third Sunday in Advent, Jubilate Sunday. All letters are black. 2. White may be used for the background with a blue or violet candle base. If violet is selected then use pink for the candle on Jubilate Sunday. Use white for the letters or black if the contrast is better when viewed from the back of the church.

ALTERNATE USE: The following samples illustrate how the flame emblem and wording from other banners in this book can be combined to form new banners for various themes.

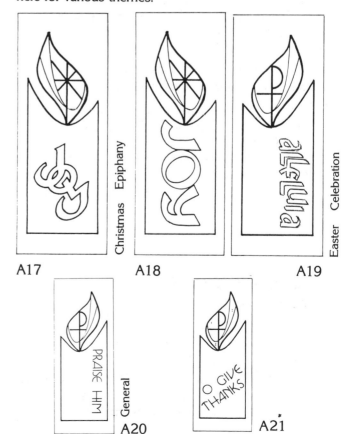

A17   Christmas   Epiphany   A18   Easter   Celebration   A19

A20   General

A21

96

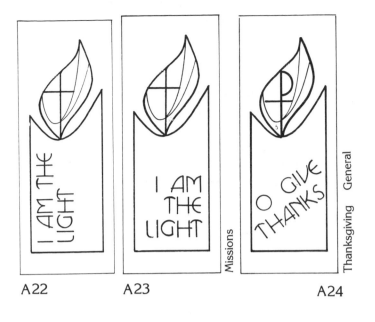

A22   A23   A24

By altering the flame emblem as illustrated more mix and match banners can be created.

A25   A26   A27

A28   A29

ALTERNATIVE CONFIRMATION BAPTISM

+ + ABIDE
IN CHRIST
ALWAYS +

THE GIFT
OF FAITH +

GROW + + +
IN CHRIST

+ + TODAY
GOD SPOKE
MY NAME +

GROW + + +
IN CHRIST

+ + ABIDE
IN CHRIST +
ALWAYS +

CONFIRMED
IN CHRIST +

BE + + +
FAITHFUL

17 Advent Candles

SUGGESTION: Use 100% polyester craft felt for the circles (halos) and flames.

SYMBOLISM: The four candles herald the four Sundays of Advent. The words are taken from the attendant pericopes. The cross, the red berries, and the thorns of the holly leaves bring to mind the suffering of Jesus when He shed His blood for the forgiveness of sins. Long ago people awaited His promised salvation and now anticipate His second coming.

18 Christmas Lamb

SUGGESTION: Use white wooly fabric for the lamb.

ALTERNATE WORDING: Allow a space as indicated on the design between the words *PEACE ON EARTH,* or *GOOD NEWS.*

SYMBOLISM: The sacrificial Lamb of God (Jesus), the Star of David, and the shepherd's crook (lineage of Christ) are symbols which point to the fulfillment of the Old Testament prophesies. The shepherd's staff also represents the shepherds who came to worship the newborn King.

ALTERNATE USE: General/Lent—Use for those pericopes that refer to the Good Shepherd, the Lamb of God, or Old Testament prophecies concerning Jesus as the descendant of King David.

19 Christmas Angel

SUGGESTION: Use 100% polyester craft felt for the angel.

ALTERNATE COLORS: The background could also be very dark or navy blue. The blue chosen must provide high contrast with the white and blend well with the yellow stars and blues used in the foreground. Experiment with gold or silver fabric, trim, or foil paper for the horn and stars. Do not use both gold and silver on the same banner.

SYMBOLISM: The seven crosses (stars) show that Christ's salvation had come to God's creation.

20 Christmas Joy

SUGGESTION: The vertical black line connecting the O's in *JOY* is optional.

SYMBOLISM: The three *JOY*s are a reminder of the Triune God. Christ (Chi-Rho, the first two letters in the Greek word) is the Light of the world (star and flame). The red berries (blood) and holly thorns (suffering) reiterate the purpose of Christ's coming to earth (the cross).

ALTERNATE USE: Celebration/general—Reduce the size of the banner to 27″ x 40″. Keep the border and include the three *JOY*s. Use the Chi-Rho in the middle

O or fill all three *O*'s from top to bottom with the symbols illustrated below. For a subtle effect on a white background use ¼" strips of soft, white felt for the outline of the symbols. This idea works best on a banner for a small church.

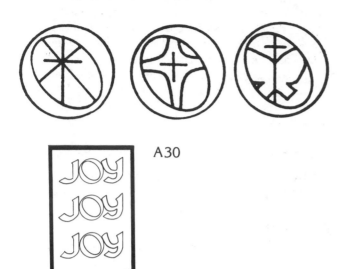

A30

These symbolize Christ's salvation as seen in Christmas (star), Lent (cross), and Easter (butterfly). This banner can be hung for one Sunday or more in each of those three seasons.

21, 22, 23 Matching Banner Sets for Christmas, Lent, and Easter

SUGGESTION: If using this set of banners more than once attach the violet and yellow circles with double stick tape. The long narrow banner (6" x 44") is referred to as a ban.

21 *HE CAME* **Banner** (set of two):

Use during the Christmas season. Alternately the ban may have a black background with blue (21) for the words and star.

SYMBOLISM: The blue semi-circle holds the hope of Jesus' coming. The star symbolically announces, *HE CAME!* Christ is the star that came from Jacob (Numbers 24:17).

22 *HE DIED* **Banner** (set of three):

Use any time during Lent, possibly Holy Week. Alternately the ban may have a black background with violet (16) for the words and cross.

SYMBOLISM: Violet is the color of sorrow and sin. Christ died (cross) to save all from sin.

23 *HE LIVES* **Banner** (set of four):

Use this set of banners for Easter. Alternately the ban may have a black background with yellow (1) for the words and butterfly.

SYMBOLISM: The yellow circle at the bottom of the banner looks like the rising sun of Easter morning. Jesus rose from the dead (butterfly-cross).

24, 25 Coordinated Christmas/ Easter Angels

The designs tie the two seasons of Christmas and Easter together. God's messengers were sent on both occasions to announce the good news.

SUGGESTION: Use 100% polyester felt for the angel figures and attach them with double stick carpet tape. To ensure stability tack the free hand and the very top part of the two wings to the background with needle and thread. When the banner is in storage pin the extra angel (if there is one) to the back of the banner. Any extra letters are placed in a ziplock bag and pinned to the back of the banner also.

ALTERNATE COLORS: It is possible to use the same angel and background for both the Christmas and Easter banners. Just substitute the stars for the crosses and use the matching wording. The blue or violet colors would be appropriate to use for either season. If making two separate banners then use the blues for Christmas and the violets for Easter.

SYMBOLISM: The Christmas angel declares the good news of the Savior's birth and the star repeats the message. The empty cross alongside the Easter angel proclaims His victory over death.

26 New Year's Blessing

SUGGESTION: Use 100% polyester felt. The bottom message area must be dark enough to provide good contrast to the light upper area of the rays and hand. Black permanent marker can be used for the lines on this part of the banner.

SYMBOLISM: Blue is the color of hope which Christians place in God's promise to care for them every day (the seven stars representing the days of the week). The double swirl with no beginning or end is at once God's omnipotence and omnipresence. The hand of blessing is centered above the words of the Benediction.

ALTERNATE USE: General/wedding/farewell.

27 Epiphany Crown

SUGGESTION: Try using foil paper, mylar, or metallic fabric for the violet of the crown. Experiment with gold metallic trim. It can be applied to the inner lines of the star and crown depending on the type and width used. If not using gold trim on the star then draw a violet (16) shade line with a felt marker or oil crayon as indicated on the design.

SYMBOLISM: Rays from the star form the manger. The crown resting in the manger represents the newborn King and the kings who came to honor Him. Violet is the color of royalty.

ALTERNATE USE: Christmas.

28 Epiphany Town

SUGGESTION: Use 100% polyester felt for the star and town.

ALTERNATE COLORS: The whole sky can be dark blue (25) with the lines extending from the points of the stars made of white rug yarn, ¼″ soft, white felt strips, or ¼″ white ribbon.

SYMBOLISM: The light blue areas look like highways, suggesting the travel of the Wise Men at the time of Christ's birth. The repetition of three colors symbolizes the Trinity. The cross in the central star hovers over Bethlehem where the Savior of the world was born.

29 Ash Wednesday Cross

SUGGESTION: There is no need to use black yarn between the dark purple and the light violet.

SYMBOLISM: The verse is taken from the pericopes for Ash Wednesday. Violet (color for Lent) indicates sorrow for the sins that put Jesus on the cross. The thorns reinforce the earthly reality of Jesus' suffering. The sunrise of Easter morning appears in the background showing the completion of God's promise of salvation for all people.

ALTERNATE USE: Lent.

30 Lent Lamb

SUGGESTION: Use white wooly fabric for the lamb. OPTIONAL COLORS: Use a gold cross with a yellow (2) satin halo and a combination of purple (20) and gold trim for the circle's outline.

SYMBOLISM: The halo distinguishes the lamb as Christ. The Lamb of God was sacrificed on the cross for the forgiveness of all sins. Violet represents the sorrow and suffering of the Lenten season.

ALTERNATE USE: Use on those Sundays on which the pericopes or sermon refers to Jesus as the Lamb of God. Check with the minister.

31 Lent/Good Friday Golgotha

SUGGESTION: Use ribbon for the lines of the cross and flexible gold metallic trim for the three circles. Glue the lines first, then the circles. Or, drape and loop ¼″ wide, gold ribbon in three intertwining circles. Allow the center of the loop to gap ½″ or less from the surface of the banner. Use dots of glue to hold the loops in place.

SYMBOLISM: The black background (death and sin) carries a red cross and horizontal band (the blood of Jesus shed for the remission of sins). The three gold circles represent the crown of thorns. The repeated use of three lines parallels the three days before Jesus will be alive again.

ALTERNATE USE: This banner's background may serve as the base for a series of quotations, e.g., the seven last words of Jesus from the cross. By using double stick tape on the back of the letters, the wording can be changed each week. Key words from sermon texts or Lenten hymns may also be used and changed as needed. Allow enough extra length at the bottom for the banner to accommodate both short and long texts and pin excess fabric to the back when using the shorter phrases.

32 Palm Sunday Hosanna

SUGGESTION: Use identical gems or craft trim to fill the four circles on the crown.

SYMBOLISM: The encircling palm branches and the crown represent Christ as king. The Chi (X)-Rho (P), first two letters in the Greek word for Christ, is part of the crown emblem. The large circle symbolizes the Kingdom of God which is without end.

ALTERNATE USE: Confirmation—Use the optional wording BE FAITHFUL.

33 Palm Sunday/ Confirmation Palm Branch

SUGGESTION: For confirmation use Ban 60 (one ban for each confirmand) along with this banner as shown. Three alternate mottos for Palm Sunday are also illustrated. To convert the banner, simply change the words attached with doublestick tape.

SYMBOLISM: The palm branch used to praise the King is bent around a red cross thus forming a shepherd's crook. A person enters God's Kingdom through faith in Christ the Savior (cross). The Good Shepherd promises to care for that person until he or she enters the eternal Kingdom of Heaven.

34 Maundy Thursday/Communion Bread and Wine (A)

SUGGESTION: Use a white brocade or heavy satin sheen drapery material for the background. Orange-yellow (3) or gold trim is optional for the border. A golden yellow fringe (approximately 3″ wide) would be attractive along the bottom of the banner.

SYMBOLISM: The bread (wafer circle) and wine (chalice) are shown in combination with the natural elements of wheat and grapes. The red cross symbolizes the blood of Jesus shed for the forgiveness of sins.

35 Maundy Thursday/Communion Bread and Wine (B)

SUGGESTION: The mottos, both reassuring to the worshiper, are made interchangeable by the use of double stick tape.

SYMBOLISM: The stalk of grain and cluster of grapes are used in combination with the wafer (circle) and chalice symbolizing the body and blood of Christ. The violet color indicates remorse while the white represents the cleansing of sins through the death of Jesus.

36 Easter Sunrise

SUGGESTION: Enlarge the word *ALLELUIA* based on the pattern as illustrated or freehand using calligraphy. The thickest part of the lines for each letter should not exceed ½".

SYMBOLISM: The Easter morning sunrise and the green bands of new life burst forth from the empty cross with the good news of Christ's victory over sin and death. The three *ALLELUIA*s and three bands of color echo to fill the emptiness felt during the three days from the cross to the resurrection.

37 Easter Lily

SUGGESTION: Use 100% polyester felt for the Easter lily blossom.

ALTERNATE WORDING: The words from Banners 39, 40 (a), and 40(b) may be substituted. Use only one *REJOICE* from Banner 40(a) and add 4" to the bottom of the banner. The motto may be changed each Sunday during the Easter season or yearly by using double stick tape to attach the letters.

SYMBOLISM: The brilliant Easter morning sun overwhelms the empty cross of Christ's suffering and death. The lily, springing from the earth in which He was buried, carries with it the promise of new life.

38 Easter Message

ALTERNATE WORDING: The banner becomes more versatile if the letters are attached with double stick tape. Substitute the script from Banner 36, Banner 39 (use *ALLELUIA* three times and lengthen the banner another 2"), or Banner 40 (use two magenta (17) *ALLELUIA*s or *REJOICE*s). If the banner is hung for several consecutive Sundays or years then the message, based on hymn titles, sermon themes, or Bible verses, may be different each time it is displayed. Consult the minister.

SYMBOLISM: Just as a butterfly emerges from its cocoon so Christ rose from the grave. The butterfly, embodying new life coming from apparent death, is

superimposed with a cross representing Christ's resurrection.

ALTERNATE USE: Funeral.

39 Easter Lilies

SUGGESTION: Use 100% polyester felt for the lilies. Enlarge the word *ALLELUIA* along with the rest of the design or do the word freehand using calligraphy.

ALTERNATE WORDING: The motto from Banner 37 or the *ALLELUIA* from Banner 40(b) may be used instead of the *ALLELUIA* on this banner.

SYMBOLISM: The symbolism for this banner is the same as for Banner 37.

40(a) Easter Butterfly
40(b) Easter Butterfly Alternate

SYMBOLISM: The cross joined with the butterfly shows the intimate relationship between Christ's death and His resurrection.

41 Easter Resurrected Christ

SUGGESTION: Use 100% polyester felt for the Christ figure and halo.

ALTERNATE COLORS: 1. Choose a light blue (21, 22, or 23) for the background to go with black letters and border. Be sure the blue contrasts strongly with the white. Experiment with gold metallic trim for the black border. 2. Have a white background with red and black letters. Make the figure of Jesus all white with a bold black outline drawn with a permanent marker. Omit the shade lines. The halo may be gold metallic paper, mylar, or fabric. The border in that case could be red with gold metallic trim. The three crosses may be metallic red or gold outlined with black rug yarn.

SYMBOLISM: Jesus rises from the conquered grave with a gesture beckoning all to accept the salvation that He won for them.

ALTERNATE USE: Missions/general/Ascension Sunday—Use the following arrangements of words.

I WILL	*MAKE*	*GO*	*PREACH*
BE WITH	*DISCIPLES*	*INTO*	*THE*
YOU	*OF ALL*	*ALL THE*	*GOOD NEWS*
ALWAYS	*NATIONS*	*WORLD*	

Funeral

Transfiguration Sunday—Make a white banner with black lines only, using gold for the halo and borders, and the motto:

THIS
IS MY SON
LISTEN TO
HIM

42 Pentecost Entering Dove

SUGGESTION: Use bright (almost orange) red for the best possible contrast to the black.

SYMBOLISM: The flame and the dove are set in an architectural opening suggesting the entrance of the Holy Spirit into the worshiper's life.

43 Pentecost Gifts

SYMBOLISM: Extending from the dove's halo are nine flames which correspond to the nine gifts of the Holy Spirit listed below. The cross in each flame represents the centrality of Christ in each one of these attributes.

44 Trinity Sunday Hand In Dove

ALTERNATE COLORS: 1. Use a white background (possibly brocade or satin sheen) with a black emblem and red (14 or 15) letters. 2. Put a red emblem with black letters on a white background. 3. Make everything but the background black or red. 4. A red background with white emblem and letters would look striking with a gold border.

SYMBOLISM: The hand (Father), Chi-Rho (Christogram) and dove (Holy Spirit) are simultaneously dependent and interdependent.

ALTERNATE USE: General/baptism—This banner is appropriate for baptism because it is a reminder that the person is baptized in the name of the Father, the Son, and the Holy Spirit. Note the addition of these words to the banner (A31). Alternate colors would be red (14) or gold metallic trim crosses, black emblem, white background, and red words.

A31

45 Trinity Sunday Geometry

SYMBOLISM: The symbols for the Triune God (as for Banner 44) are set within a geometric framework. The blues suggest the hope that is placed in God's promises.

BANNERS FOR SPECIFIC OCCASIONS

46 Thanksgiving Radiance

ALTERNATE WORDING:	*PRAISE HIM*	*PRAISE GOD*

SYMBOLISM: The dominant sun with its radiating light represents the easily recognizable, daily physical blessings for which the worshiper gives thanks. The cross repeated three times shows the continuity of the more important spiritual gifts received from the Lord through the Word (book—Bible) and Sacraments (shell—baptism, wafer and chalice—communion).

ALTERNATE USE: General/confirmation—Use the wording
GROW IN CHRIST

47 Thanksgiving Seasons

SYMBOLISM: The seasons (snowflake—winter, tulip—spring, butterfly—summer, golden leaf—autumn) revolve around the cross of Christ showing physical blessings centered on spiritual ones.

ALTERNATE USE: General/celebration—Use to celebrate the years of service a church worker has given.

48 Baptism Water Drops

SUGGESTION: This banner may be used as a gift for the baptized.

ALTERNATE BANNER: This banner can be made without the emblem. If so, then reduce its total length to 26″ and consider making a border. The letters can be fashioned from a highly contrasting solid color such as blue, red, or green, or even from a fabric with a small print. The bottom of the banner might have a self- or matching fringe.

49 Baptism Gift

SUGGESTION: The width of the banner will vary according to the length of the person's name. This banner may be used as a gift for the baptized. Use corduroy for the blue (24) portion of the shell. Cut the outline of the blue shell ¼″ smaller. Rub glue over the raw edge to check the fuzzing of the material. Glue the lined, white portion of the emblem to the corduroy so the ribbing is vertical.

ALTERNATE BANNER: 1. Use the simpler alternate emblem in place of the shell. 2. It is possible to eliminate the emblem altogether and reduce the length of the banner to 28″. The wording and optional border can be any bright, contrasting color, e.g., red, blue, or green. A fabric with small print will work here as well. The bottom of the banner can have a self- or harmonizing fringe.

SYMBOLISM: Within baptism (shell) the Holy Spirit (dove) brings the gift of faith in Christ (cross) to the person. The three crosses incorporated in the motto parallel the ceremony done in the name of the Father, Son, and Holy Spirit.

50 Baptism Dove

SUGGESTION: Use three contrasting solid blues for the drops of water.

SYMBOLISM: The Holy Spirit (dove) brings the gift of faith in Jesus (cross) to the person. The cross is centered in the three drops of water used to baptize in the name of the Father, Son, and Holy Spirit.

51 Baptism Shell

SYMBOLISM: The Holy Spirit brings the gift of faith in Jesus (Chi-Rho—the first two letters in the Greek word for Christ) through baptism in which the person is washed (blue—water) of sin and made holy (halo).

52 Baptism Candle

ALTERNATE WORDING: One of the five alternate mottos may be used to fill the white candlestick. Arrange the words in block form as illustrated. The crosses may be red trim or gold, if it can be seen from a distance.

SYMBOLISM: The three shades of blue (the color of hope for eternal life in heaven) in the flame bring to mind the three drops of water used to baptize in the name of the Triune God.

53–60 Baptism/Confirmation Bans

Bans are long narrow banners containing a caption and/or simple emblem. These bans may be presented to the baptized or confirmed after the ceremony. Bans 53–60 can all be used for baptism and Bans 58–60 are also especially suitable for confirmation. By mixing and matching the mottos and emblems, more confirmation and baptism bans can be formed. These bans can be used alone or along with other baptism or confirmation banners.

SUGGESTION: Bans 53, 55, 57, 58, 59, and 60 may have a flat rather than a slanted bottom. A ban's length depends upon the name and motto chosen. If the bans for a particular confirmation class are all the same design, then make them all the same length (de-

termined by the longest name), too. Permanent black marker can be used to draw the emblems and the letters from Linear Alphabet B directly on 100% polyester felt. If the finished ban is light enough, use a plastic straw trimmed to the width of the ban as the rod. Yarn or cord can then be strung through the straw and the knot pulled inside.

SYMBOLISM FOR BANS 53–60:

Ban 53: The Holy Spirit (dove) brings the gift of faith to the baptized.

Ban 54: As the leaf grows attached to the cross so may the baptized grow in faith in Christ.

Ban 55: A person is baptized (shell) into Christ (cross).

Ban 56: The Holy Spirit (dove) gives the gift of faith in Jesus (cross).

Ban 57: The three crosses centered in water drops symbolize baptism in the name of the Triune God.

Ban 58: Just as a plant grows daily in the light of the sun so the confirmed person grows daily in the love of the Son (cross).

Ban 59: The Holy Spirit (dove) abides with God's child.

Ban 60: Christ is both Savior (cross) and Good Shepherd (crook) who promises to care for each of His children.

61 Confirmation Candle

SYMBOLISM: The Holy Spirit (flame/dove) continually helps the confirmand to live a life of love and obedience to Christ (cross).

ALTERNATE USE: Baptism—Change the red to blue (24) and *CONFIRMED* to *BAPTIZED*.

62 Confirmation Cross-Crook

SYMBOLISM: Just as the bright sun nourishes the plant so the Holy Spirit nourishes the faith of the believer. The Lord who is the Good Shepherd (crook) promises to care for His children. He offers forgiveness (cross) and life eternal to all believers including the confirmand (the leaf attached to the cross-crook).

ALTERNATE USE: Baptism.

63 Confirmation Vine

SUGGESTION: For an unusual effect embroider the emblem with yarn (fabric could be used for the larger areas of color).

SYMBOLISM: The base of the serpentine vine contains the work of the Holy Spirit. Here at confirmation, the dove renews the flame of faith that springs from the vessel containing the blue waters of baptism. In the middle loop, the Christian continues to grow in his faith through communion (chalice and wafer) and extends the love of Christ to others (cross-fish hook=fishers of men). In the top portion of the vine the Bible offers the promise of new life with God in heaven after death (butterfly).

64 Confirmation Circle

SUGGESTION: The banner may have a border in red, green, or black.

SYMBOLISM: The Holy Spirit (dove) who gives the gift of faith in Jesus (cross) continues to nurture that faith as symbolized by the green leaf stemming from the cross.

ALTERNATE USE: Baptism—The wording may be changed.

65 Confirmation Crown

SYMBOLISM: The thought is taken from Revelation 2:10. The Triune God (hand—Father, cross—Son, and dove—Holy Spirit) promises the crown of life to those who remain faithful.

ALTERNATE USE: Trinity Sunday—Change the motto to fit the occasion. The crown could symbolize the Kingdom of God or Christ as King.

66 Confirmation Ban and Banner Set

SUGGESTION: The colored ban on the left side of the banner is a separate piece carefully hung to look like part of the larger banner. Red is the suggested color but any color that matches one of the other colors on the banner may be used. If the banner is hung for consecutive years, then make the ban a different color each year and change the message on the ban as well. A border ribbon of the same color as the ban can be taped (use double stick tape) over the red border indicated in the original design. Alternate wording might be *CHRIST LIVES IN ME, JOY JOY JOY,* or *I'VE GOT THE JOY.*

SYMBOLISM: The Holy Spirit (dove) gives faith to each person (leaf rooted in the base of the staff) in baptism (blue drops of water on the leaf). The Holy Spirit continues to sanctify (flames) and help the confirmand live a life of love and obedience to the Good Shepherd-Redeemer (staff and cross).

67 Wedding Rainbow

SYMBOLISM: The rainbow foretells a bright future. The two doves and interlocked wedding rings touching the cross symbolize the promise a couple makes before God to love each other until death parts them.

68 Wedding Hearts

SYMBOLISM: The two doves and intertwined hearts centered around a cross indicate a wedding couple who desire to have Christ as the center of their life together.

ALTERNATE BANNERS: The circle emblems of Banners 70–72 and the rings emblem of Banner 75 may be used in place of the hearts. Make the banner 40″ long, allowing 3″ between the top of the emblem and the top edge of the banner and 5″ between the words and the bottom of the banner. The wording may be changed as desired.

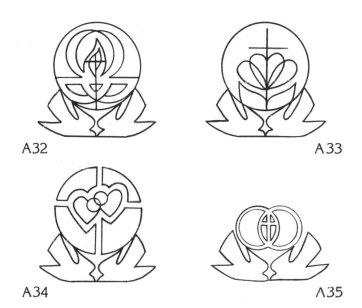

A32
A33
A34
A35

69 Wedding Candle

SUGGESTION: The repeated word *REJOICE* can be any combination of colors such as those suggested for Banners 9–12 and Banner 100. The words and upper portion of the background may be one of the colors worn by the wedding party. Be sure the color chosen provides enough contrast to the white of the candle. If this banner is kept by the church then consider using colors for the words and upper background that match the paraments. If the season is white then use something else.

SYMBOLISM: All rejoice with the wedding couple in their commitment to love each other and to have Christ the center of their marriage.

ALTERNATE WORDING: Position the word *JOY* on the candle as in Banner A28 or A29. Or extend the vertical line of the cross to the bottom of the banner and place the couple's names on both sides of the line as in Banner 76.

70–75 Wedding Series
70 Wedding Hearts

SUGGESTION: All the lines of the emblem and the letters are outlined with black rug yarn. The line for the circle around the emblem can be black or gold metallic trim or both depending on the width and visibility of the trim used. The emblem can be used without the circle outline. The emblem is interchangeable with the emblems on Banners 68 (A34), 71, and 72. If substituting use double stick carpet tape to attach the circle emblem. **Note how the design changes depending on how it is colored.**

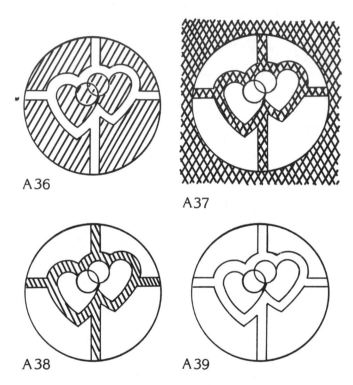

A36

A37

A38

A39

SUGGESTED COLORS: 1. Have an all white banner with black outlining and possibly a gold metallic border. 2. Use colors that match the paraments for the season. 3. Use the color worn by the wedding party for the border, emblem, and word. If they are wearing two colors use the brighter hue for the emblem and the border. There must be a strong enough contrast between the colors and the white background to make the emblem and words visible from a distance.

SYMBOLISM: The two hearts are made one in the cross showing that Christ binds the couple together.

71 Wedding Flames

SUGGESTION: A border can be added to the banner. The emblem can be used without the circle outline. The emblem is interchangeable with the emblems of Banners 68 (A32), 70, and 72. If switching the circle emblems use double stick carpet tape to attach them to the banner.

SUGGESTED COLORS: Use orange-yellow (3) or ochre (4) for the lamp-flame portion of the design. For other color selections refer to Banner 70.

SYMBOLISM: The two oil lamps combine to form one flame centered on the cross. The light's double halo resembles the rings exchanged in the ceremony.

72 Wedding Flower

SUGGESTION: The emblem is interchangeable with those shown on Banners 70 and 71. If substituting emblems use double stick carpet tape for attachment. A rose (13) border can be added to the banner.

SYMBOLISM: The cross is central to the growing plant which blossoms around it. The flower is actually two independent hearts, one on each side of the cross-stem, joining together to form a third, single (deeper pink) heart.

73 Heart-Cross Emblem

SUGGESTION: These intertwined hearts can be used for Banners 70–72. Refer to Banner 70 for alternate color schemes. A border of matching or harmonizing color can be used. The circle lines are optional.

SYMBOLISM: The fusing of two hearts into one unending loop shows the joining of two people into one in marriage. Their commitment to each other is centered in Christ (cross) who supports them with His love.

74 Doves Emblem

SUGGESTION: This emblem works well on Banners 70–72; use double stick tape to attach it if interchangeability is desired. The banner may consist of all black lines on a white background. The circle may be omitted. A border of matching and harmonizing color may be used.

SYMBOLISM: The bilaterally symmetrical arrangement of the hearts and doves under the cross suggests the perfection of married love in Christ.

75 Rings Emblem

SUGGESTION: The design may consist of all black lines on a white background. Use Wonder-Under to fuse the design pieces to the background. Made in satin, this banner becomes an unusual wall hanging for the home.

ALTERNATE BANNERS: The rings and dove can be substituted for any of the emblems on Banners 70–72.

SYMBOLISM: The blessings of God (dove) abide in a Christ-centered marriage (cross within the rings).

76 Wedding Candle With Names

SUGGESTION: The length of the banner may be determined by the names used; however, do not make the banner shorter than indicated. Deep yellow (2) is used for the whole flame with black rug yarn or felt for the lines within the emblem. Use black ribbon to outline the sides of the candle and black rug yarn for the curve on the top of the candle.

SYMBOLISM: Two names, two rings, and two crosses are united in one brightly burning flame of married love.

ALTERNATE USE: Anniversary celebration—The anniversary year (3″ numerals) may be placed in the upper left-hand corner.

77 Wedding Seagulls and Sunshine

SYMBOLISM: The two seagulls in flight against a dominant sun suggest the wedding couple blessed each day of their lives by a caring Lord.

ALTERNATE USE: New Year's Eve/Day—For this celebration the sun and seagulls in flight embody the daily presence of the Lord in Christians' lives.

78 Wedding Bands

SUGGESTION: The colors within the two overlapping wedding bands can be changed. Use white in the two central areas (marked gold on the design) and another color in the four surrounding areas. If using some other color besides white or gold in the two centers make sure that it is lighter and brighter than the color in the surrounding areas. A border matching or harmonizing with any color in the banner may be used. The black lines should be ¼″ or ⅜″ wide. If using 100% polyester felt, the lines and words can be drawn on with a permanent black felt-tip marker.

SYMBOLISM: Two people coming together in marriage (overlapping rings) become one in the Lord (double lines forming a cross).

ALTERNATE USE: Anniversary celebration—The anniversary year (3″ numerals) may be placed in the upper right-hand corner.

All of the wedding banners can also be used to celebrate anniversaries.

79–85 Christian Life Series

This set of banners may be used singly or as a group. Each deals with a portion of the Christian experience beginning with baptism and ending with the hope for eternal life. If a motto is desired then enlarge the background to accommodate the words, or, try alternate background shapes and bans to carry the words. Use double stick tape to attach the letters if the words are to be changed.

ALTERNATE DESIGNS: Either the cross or cross/shepherd's staff may be used in the emblems for Banners 79—84 depending on the emphasis desired.

SYMBOLISM FOR BANNERS 79–85: All the banners use a set of green leaves (growth) attached to the base of a cross or staff-cross. This shows that a Christian life is rooted in and nurtured by the love of Christ. The cross stands for the universal salvation offered by Jesus, and the cross-shepherd's staff emphasizes Jesus' care for the individual Christian.

SYMBOLISM FOR EACH BANNER:

79 BAPTISM: Baptism in the name of the Triune God is symbolized by the three bands of water. The descending dove (Holy Spirit) imparts its blessings at this beginning of the Christian life.

80 CHRISTIAN EDUCATION: The person grows in faith through study of the Word (oil lamp).

81 CONFIRMATION: The Holy Spirit continues to sanctify the confirmed Christian.

82 COMMUNION: The bread (wheat) and wine (grapes) are the visible elements used in the Lord's supper for the forgiveness of sins and strengthening of faith.

83 MARRIAGE AND FAMILY: The linked rings show a couple's bond of love.

84 MISSIONS: Christ commanded His followers to be fishers of men (hook-cross) and to go into all the world with the good news of Jesus Christ. The leaves form the fish sign which was used by the early Christians to identify themselves as followers of Christ.

85 DEATH/RESURRECTION: The blue cross-anchor is the symbol of hope for eternal life in heaven after death. The butterfly is the symbol for resurrection from the dead. This banner may also be used for Easter or a funeral.

ALTERNATE USE: Installation of church worker—Add an appropriate text to Banner 80 or 84.

86–99 Joy Series

Banner 86, the basic design, demonstrates the correct position of the flame or leaf variations above the word *JOY* in the rest of the series. Each emblem is made interchangeable by using double stick tape on the back. Banners may be used singly or as part of any desired combination.

SUGGESTION: Outline the word *JOY* and the leaf design with black rug yarn or ¼″ soft, black felt strips. If the background is dark then there is no need to outline. Any combination of colors may be used for the word *JOY* and the flame/leaf emblem. Always make sure the colors harmonize, fit in with the color symbolism for the occasion, and have high contrast. Experiment by making several tracings of the emblem and use markers or crayons for developing an eye-pleasing color combination. If using 2 or 3 colors place the color of highest value in the inner most area of the flame/leaf. Other words may be added to the chosen design; enlarge the background accordingly. The banner as illustrated measures 18″ x 27″. By using the scale of ¼″ equal to 3″ the banner is enlarged to 27″ x 40.5″ with the central design's dimensions of 18″ x 28.5″.

ALTERNATE BACKGROUND SHAPE: Note all of the three piece background shapes which may be used for the design. Words and short phrases may be used on the side bans as illustrated (A3).

BANNER'S TITLE, ALTERNATE COLORS (indicated in parentheses), **SYMBOLISM, AND ALTERNATE USE:**

86 LIGHT: Use *JOY* (1) on a black or royal blue background with the inner part of the flame (1) and the outer portion (5). Use as a general banner symbolizing Christ as the Light of the world. Or use for missions in which the worshiper is to be a light to others.

86 PENTECOST: Use *JOY* (W) on a red (14) background with the inner part of flame the yellow of the first Pentecost (2), and outer part of flame (W). Experiment with gold trim between the white and yellow areas.

87 GROWTH: Use (8) for *JOY* and the outer part of the leaf and (9 or 10) for the inner leaf on a black background. Or put *JOY* (9 or 10) on a white background. The green leaf symbolizes growth in the life of a Christian. Use for general occasions or Christian education.

88 CHRISTMAS/EPIPHANY: Make *JOY* and outer flame area (W) and have the inner area and background a deep blue (24 or 25). The star has white lines. Experiment with gold trim on the flame. The star is that which led the way to the newborn King; or Christ is the star that brought light to the world.

89 CHI-RHO: Use white for the background and for the inner part of the flame and any color, such as the color of the paraments, for the outer part of the flame and the word *JOY*. Chi (X) and Rho (P) are the first two letters in the Greek word for Christ. Use for general occasions (greens), Transfiguration Sunday (white with gold trim on a deep blue background), Ascension Sunday (blues on white background), or a church season such as Advent (violets or blues with white).

90 PALM SUNDAY: The palm leaf was used to hail Jesus as King.

91 COMMUNION: Use *JOY* (3) if the contrast is strong enough to the white background. The wheat and grapes represent the bread and wine used in communion.

92 LENT: The Christian rejoices in the gift of forgiveness and salvation given through Christ's suffering and death (violet) on the cross. This banner may be used generally; the colors may vary according to the season or occasion.

93 EASTER: *JOY* and the butterfly may be bright Easter colors that contrast well with each other and the white background, for example, yellow and violet, two turquoise blues, or two bright violets. Use the lighter value color for the central part of the butterfly. Enlarge the banner and allow 3″ of empty space at the top and sides and 5″ at the bottom. The leaf doubled upon a cross forms a butterfly symbolizing the resurrection.

94 HOLY SPIRIT: Enlarge the banner allowing 3″ of empty space at the top and sides and 5″ at the bottom. The dove stands for the Holy Spirit. This may be used for baptism (use blue (21 or 24) for the dove's outline and *JOY*), confirmation, Pentecost, or general occasions.

95 BAPTISM: The three crosses show how baptism is done in the name of the Triune God. Use red (14) for *JOY* and the outer part of the flame and white for the background and inner flame.

96 WORD: Make *JOY* and the outer part of the flame (14) on a white background. Or make *JOY* and the outer part of the flame (2) and the inner area of the leaf (W) on a black background. This banner is suited for general or education themes and recalls Psalm 119:105.

97 FISH: Make *JOY* and the outer leaf (21), inner leaf (B), and the fish (W) on a black background. The fish brings to mind the portion of scripture where Christ tells His followers to be fishers of men. Use this idea for mission emphasis. Fish, in Greek an acronym for Jesus Christ Son of God Savior, was used by the Early Christians to identify each other, so this banner may also serve for general use.

98 GOOD SHEPHERD: The staff is a reminder of the Good Shepherd who laid down His life for His sheep (cross). Use this banner for Good Shepherd Sunday. It may also be used for the ordination or installation of a minister. The design then can be seen to show the care he is expected to give to his portion of God's flock. The colors for *JOY* and the emblem may be the same as the colors in the paraments being used.

99 WEDDING/ANNIVERSARY: Use one of the colors worn by the wedding party for the two flames/leaves. If the emblem is a flame then use a highly contrasting yellow or metallic gold. If the emblem is a set of leaves then use a medium green. The wedding couple (the comingled flames or leaves) are bonded together by Christ (cross).

ALTERNATE USE: Installation of church worker—Use Banners 87, 96–98 with an appropriate text.

100 Alleluia Chorus

SUGGESTION: Experiment with five different colors for the five ALLELUIAs. One color may be used for all five words.

SYMBOLISM: The repeated word expresses unending praise for all that God is.

ALTERNATE USE: Easter, general, or any occasion of celebration.

101 Installation of Church Worker Lamp

SUGGESTION: One or both side bans may be used with the banner. The letters for the word GLORIA may be outlined in black.

SYMBOLISM: Matthew 5:16 is the source of the banner's thought. The church worker as a called servant of the Lord is a shining light (the flame from the lamp) that proclaims the good news of Salvation (the empty, open cross) so that all may give God glory (the golden rays).

ALTERNATE USE: Ordination, confirmation, Christian education—Use during the summer months of the Pentecost season or at a Sunday school rally. Change the text to YOUR WORD IS A LAMP UNTO MY FEET. Place the text in two rows of (white) words on one larger green side ban.

102 Installation/Ordination Flock of Crosses

ALTERNATE COLORS: Use the color of the season (check a liturgical calendar) for the background and use white for the emblem lines and the letters. If white is the color of the background use black lines for the emblem and red for the small crosses and the words.

SYMBOLISM: In ministering, the Word (made flesh to bring salvation to all—large cross) and Sacraments (baptism—dove, communion—chalice and wafer) are offered (hands) to the community of souls (small crosses) for their comfort and growth in(to) faith.

ALTERNATE USE: Missions— Substitute the word BRING for the word PREACH. The small crosses become those who are brought the good news of salvation and nurtured in their new faith through the Word and Sacraments.

103 Installation of Church Worker Lamb

SUGGESTION: This banner can be personalized by reducing it to a smaller version (A4, A5). The name of the person called to serve the church in some way is put at the top of the banner. The banner may be given to the individual as a gift to be hung at home, office, or classroom. Widen the banner if necessary to accommodate the width of the person's name. The bottom may have a self-fringe. The background may be the liturgical color of the season using either black or white letters and staff. The staff may be brown if it contrasts and harmonizes well with the background.

SYMBOLISM: The Good Shepherd laid down His life that all might belong to His fold (cross-staff). Christ commands those who are called to serve Him to nurture and care for His flock (lamb inside the heart).

ALTERNATE USE: Ordination of a minister, commissioning of a church officer, teacher, or leader. If it has to do with leading or teaching children then use the word LAMBS rather than SHEEP on the banner.

104 General Radiating Dove

SUGGESTION: Make removable letters and change the wording to suit the occasion.

SYMBOLISM: The Holy Spirit (dove) enriches the Christian's life with the many blessings of God (multicolored radiating beams).

ALTERNATE USE: Baptism, confirmation, Christian education, missions, installation of church worker.

Farewell—Substitute the words

THE LORD BLESS AND KEEP YOU.

105 General Guiding Christ

SUGGESTION: Use ⅜" soft, black felt for the lines of the Christ figure. The following ideas may be used if they enhance the banner. Try gold braid trim for the outline of the halo. Or cover the entire halo area with gold mylar or fabric and then outline it with the strip of black felt.

SYMBOLISM: Christ welcomes all people with his open arms to accept salvation (cross) through faith in Him.

ALTERNATE USE: Christ, Christian education, confirmation, funeral, or missions.

Banner Index

The banners are illustrated in the pattern section and discussed in the information section in numerical order. Alternate designs are listed here followed by the numbers of the pages where they appear. A change of wording may be necessary to make some banners suit the designated theme.

SEWING INDEX

YARDAGE CHART

INCHES	YARD
4.5	1/8
9	1/4
13.5	3/8
18	1/2
22.5	5/8
27	3/4
31.5	7/8